Is Hell Forever?

Does the Bible teach that Hell will be Annihilation or Eternal Torment?

Chris Date vs. Phil Fernandes

Table of Contents

The Case for Conditionalism
by Chris Date

Introduction

Good evening, and welcome. My name is Chris Date, and tonight I'll be representing what has come to be known as *annihilationism*, more historically known as *conditional immortality* or *conditionalism* for short, terminology I'll explain a little bit later. You can learn more about this view at www.rethinkinghell.com, and you can find our podcast in iTunes by searching for "Rethinking Hell".

I'd like to begin by thanking my friend Dr. Fernandes for accepting my invitation to debate this topic, but more so for his apologetics ministry, equipping God's people to defend our worldview from the criticisms of an increasingly hostile culture. The importance and eternal value of the work he's doing by God's grace cannot be overstated.

Most of all, I want to thank you, our readers. A formal, academic, maybe even somewhat dry debate doesn't sound all that exciting to many people, even less so when the topic of the debate is as sad and terrifying a topic as hell. But it's a topic that, while not essential to the Christian faith, does touch upon a number of very important issues: the character of God; the clarity and consistency of Scripture; and the atoning work of our Lord and Savior, Jesus Christ. So I'm thankful and encouraged that you are reading this, and I'm confident that your time will not have been wasted.

Dr. Fernandes and I are both conservative, evangelical Christians. We agree on the essentials of the faith, including doctrines like the Trinity, the deity of Christ, and salvation by faith through grace alone. And we both believe that the Bible is without error, that it is our infallible source and authoritative standard of truth.

One of the essentials of Christianity we both affirm is the resurrection of all mankind, both of the saved and of the unsaved. The resurrected bodies of believers will be transformed, from bodies that were once frail, subject to pain, disease and aging, to bodies that will be incorruptible, powerful and glorious. Theologians call this *glorification*, which also renders bodies immortal, capable of living forever.

But what about the resurrected bodies of the lost? Those who had died without forgiveness? Well this is where Dr. Fernandes and I disagree, and where tonight's debate proposition comes in, which is this: "The punishment of hell will be annihilation, the everlasting loss of life and conscious existence." I will be arguing that this statement is true, and Dr. Fernandes will be arguing that it is not.

Summary

At the core of our disagreement are those three little words, "loss of life." Like most Christians since the 3rd century or so, Dr. Fernandes thinks that when unbelievers rise from the dead, their bodies, too, will be transformed into bodies that are capable of living forever—though only to be punished with everlasting, conscious separation and isolation from God. But like many or most Christians prior to the 3rd century, I believe that when the unsaved rise from the dead, their bodies will remain every bit as mortal as they are now, and that they will instead be killed, dying a second, permanent death—*annihilation*. The difference between Dr. Fernandes' position and mine is therefore analogous to the difference between corporal punishment on the one hand, and capital punishment on the other; between an everlasting prison sentence and an irreversible execution.

Not once tonight will I suggest that God is too loving or merciful to send people to hell forever, or that eternal torment in hell isn't fair; I don't even personally feel that way. Nor will I appeal to your emotions, or to philosophy, or to Church tradition or history.

Instead, in support of my position tonight, the case I'm going to present will be a comprehensive, thematic and theological one, based on three arguments which I'm calling "The Biblical Question of Immortality," "The Biblical Nature of the Atonement," and "The Biblical Language of Destruction." (Fellow Rethinking Hell contributor Dr. Glenn Peoples coined the names for the first and third of these arguments.) While each of these three arguments is more powerful in light of the other two, each is capable of standing on its own as a powerful case for my position. What's more, each is based on a very high view of Scripture, recognizing the full trustworthiness, consistency and authority of the Bible, from start to finish.

The Biblical Question of Immortality

Only God is by nature immortal. Human beings are mortal by nature, and by default will not live forever. Immortality is not universal. They can only receive immortality on the condition that God gives it to them as a gift through Jesus Christ (*conditional immortality*), and only then will they live forever. The unsaved, therefore, will not live forever.

1 Timothy 6:15-16 tells us that it is "the King of kings and Lord of lords, who alone has immortality." It follows logically that therefore fallen human beings are not inherently immortal. And Scripture tells us that immortality is a gift given only to the saved.

This great theme of Scripture is found literally from cover to cover. In **Genesis 2:17** God tells Adam that if he eats from the forbidden tree, he "shall surely die." The warning was, "in the day that you eat of [the tree] you shall surely die," and this has led some to believe that there's some spiritual sense in which Adam and Eve "died" on the day they ate that fruit. But if true, that's only one aspect of the death God had warned about, for in **Genesis 3:22-24**, "Then the LORD God said, '…lest [the man] reach out his hand and take also of the tree of life and eat, and live forever—' therefore the LORD God sent him out from the garden of Eden," and then God guarded the way to the tree of life from them. You see, as punishment for their sin, God banished Adam and Eve from the garden and from the tree of life so that they would not live forever. And at the opposite end of the Bible, in the imagery of the closing chapters of the book of Revelation, only the saved have access to that tree of life, symbolism communicating that only they will live forever (**Rev. 22:2**).

You see, the hope of immortality, of living forever, was lost in Adam, and is found only in relationship with God. **Proverbs 12:28** says,

"In the path of righteousness is life, and in its pathway there is no death," implying that any other path brings death. **Romans 2:7** says that "to those who by patience in well-doing seek for glory and honor and immortality, [God] will give eternal life," so immortality must be sought, and will not be given to those who "do not obey the truth, [for whom] there will [instead] be wrath and fury."

Paul wrote in **2 Timothy 1:10** that "our Savior Christ Jesus…abolished death and brought life and immortality to light through the gospel." He says in **1 Corinthians 15:50-53** that the earthly, perishable, mortal bodies of the saved will be made imperishable and immortal, so that we can inherit the kingdom of God.

With this in mind, consider verses you've heard a thousand times, but whose contrast between life and death you might have overlooked. "For God so loved the world, that he gave his only Son, that whoever believes in him should not perish, but have eternal life" (**John 3:16**). "I give them eternal life, and they will never perish" (**John 10:28**). "The wages of sin is death, but the free gift of God is eternal life in Christ

Jesus our Lord" (**Romans 6:23**). Of course, Christians do die, so a truly final death must be what is overcome through faith.

So, Dr. Fernandes' view is that the unsaved will live forever, albeit in hell. As I summarized earlier, however, the answer to "The Biblical Question of Immortality" is that human beings can only receive immortality on the condition that God gives it to them as a gift through Jesus Christ. The unsaved, therefore, will not live forever.

The Biblical Nature of the Atonement

Jesus bore the punishment of hell in place of those who deserve it, as their substitute. The punishment Jesus bore was suffering and death. Therefore, those who must instead bear their own punishment will likewise be punished with suffering and death.

Dr. Fernandes and I agree that Jesus suffered, and that the risen lost will suffer. But another great theme of Scripture is the atoning, substitutionary, physical death of Christ. By *substitutionary* we mean that Jesus was our *substitute*. A substitute is a person or thing that acts or serves in place of another. Think of a substitute teacher who teaches in the place of a class' normal teacher when she's sick. Or think of a substitute pitcher who pitches in the place of a team's normal pitcher when his arm is injured. You could even think of a substitute ingredient which takes the place of a recipe's normal ingredient if someone is allergic to or dislikes the normal one. Similarly, Jesus was our substitute because he suffered our punishment in our place, so that we would not have to.

Now, consider what Dr. Fernandes correctly and repeatedly identifies as the punishment Jesus bore in our place: "Jesus died in our place and took our punishment for us as a substitute sacrifice for our sins...the ultimately worthy substitute sacrifice for our sins would come and die...God as God cannot die. Hence, in order to represent man and to be able to die as our substitute sacrifice, God the Son had to become a man...Jesus, the God-man, has paid the full price for our sins by dying on the cross. God is satisfied with Jesus' death—the ultimate price." (Fernandes, *Hijacking the Historical Jesus* (CreateSpace, 2012), 283-6.)

Dr. Fernandes is absolutely right. **Isaiah 53:5**'s famous "he was pierced for our transgressions" is followed in **verses 8-9** by "he was cut off out of the land of the living, stricken for the transgression of my people…And they made his grave with the wicked." Paul says in **Romans 5:6 and 8** that "at the right time Christ died for the ungodly," and that "God demonstrates his own love toward us, in that while we were yet sinners, Christ died for us." Paul calls this the gospel in **1 Corinthians 15:1-4**, writing, "I delivered to you as of first importance…that Christ died for our sins." In **2 Corinthians 5:15** Paul writes again of "him who for their sake died and was raised." Peter likewise says in **1 Peter 3:18**, "Christ also suffered once for sins…being put to death in the flesh."

Now, to be sure, Jesus suffered as part of his atoning death, but he also died. And so whereas Dr. Fernandes' view is that the unsaved will live forever, albeit in hell, as I summarized earlier, "The Biblical Nature of the Atonement" is that the punishment Jesus bore in our place was suffering and death. Therefore, those who must instead bear their own punishment will likewise be punished with suffering and death.

The Biblical Language of Destruction

The Bible consistently, repeatedly, in no uncertain terms and in a variety of ways, says that the fate of the unsaved will be destruction, a complete and irreversible end of life.

This certainly appears to be the unanimous Old Testament witness. Although I could spend a lot of time demonstrating this, I'll just give you a sampling from the **Psalms**, which indicate that the unsaved will: fade and wither like grass (**37:2**); be consumed, be no more (**104:35**); perish (**1:6**); vanish like smoke (**37:20**); be destroyed and cut off (**37:38**); be broken and dashed to pieces (**2:9**); be slain (**139:19**); be blotted out from the book of the living (**69:28**); be blown away like chaff (**1:4**); be like a dream forgotten when one awakens (**73:20**); melt like wax and perish (**68:2**).

Now, God's judicial, destructive wrath is not always poured out in these ways on the unrighteous in this life. Many of them die in peace and in luxury, and do not vanish from the sight of the godly; frequently it's the other way around. And so I think we have good reason to see these metaphors as principles of divine justice that will be true in the final punishment, even if not always true in the here and now.

The New Testament just as strongly foretells the final destruction of the unsaved. It does so in straightforward and didactic statements, historical events given as examples, analogies and metaphors, and symbolic imagery and visions. And some of these texts are typically cited as support for the traditional view of hell, when in fact they are stronger support for the position I'm defending tonight.

Jesus says in **Matthew 10:28**, "do not fear those who kill the body but cannot kill the soul. Rather fear him who can destroy both soul and body in hell." In **Matthew 7:13-14** he says "the gate is wide and the way is easy that leads to destruction." **Philippians 3:19** says "their end is destruction." **2 Thessalonians 1:9** says they "will suffer the punishment of eternal destruction." Numerous other examples could be cited.

Traditionally the debate has centered around the meaning of the various words translated "destroy," but when it comes to Matthew 10:28, the word here translated "destroy" consistently means something like "slay" or "kill" in the synoptic gospels, when used in the grammatical form it's used here. In **Matthew 2:13** Herod wants to kill the baby Jesus. In **Matthew 12:14** and **Mark 3:6** the Pharisees want to kill Jesus. In **Mark 9:22** a demon is said to throw its host into fire to try and kill him. There's just no reason to believe Jesus is using the word translated "destroy" differently in Matthew 10:28, than it's used in these and many other verses in the synoptic gospels, particularly in light of his contrast between men who can kill only the body but can't kill the soul, and God who can kill both in hell.

2 Peter 3:6-7 compares the future destruction of the ungodly to those killed by Noah's flood, saying that "the world that then existed was deluged with water and perished," and that the ungodly are "being kept until the day of judgment and destruction of the ungodly."

2 Peter 2:6 and **Jude 7** compare the future destruction of the ungodly to the past destruction of the people of Sodom and Gomorrah. Peter says that "by turning the cities of Sodom and Gomorrah to ashes [God] condemned them to extinction, making them an example of what is going to happen to the ungodly."

Jude calls the fire that destroyed those cities "eternal fire," which Jesus said in **Matthew 25:41-46** is the "eternal punishment" awaiting the unsaved. An eternity of ongoing punishing is not what's in view there; rather, it's the punishment of death—an eternal death from which they will never rise to life again. It's no wonder, then, that the fate of the lost is contrasted with "eternal life," for unlike the saved, they will not live forever.

Matthew 13:40-42 compares the future destruction of the unsaved to weeds being completely burned up in fire, saying, "Just as the weeds are gathered and burned with fire, so will it be at the end of the

14

age…they will gather out of his kingdom all causes of sin and all law-breakers, and thrown them into the fiery furnace. In that place there will be weeping and gnashing of teeth."

That last verse has been thought by many to be support for the traditional view of hell, but as you can see, the duration of their weeping and gnashing is limited to the time it takes to be burned up like weeds. Jesus is alluding to **Malachi 4:1 and 3** which says that "the day is coming, burning like an oven, when all the arrogant and all evildoers will be stubble. The day that is coming shall set them ablaze…and you shall tread down the wicked, for they will be ashes under the soles of your feet."

Most often misunderstood are texts which fall under the category of symbolic imagery and visions. In **Mark 9:48**, Jesus says that in hell, "their worm does not die, and the fire is not quenched," quoting **Isaiah 66:24** which says it is "the dead bodies of the men who have rebelled against Me [whose] worm shall not die [and whose] fire will not be quenched." The picture is of the corpses of God's slain enemies, being consumed by fire and maggots.

Unquenchable fire is not fire which never dies out; it's fire which can't be put out, and so irresistibly consumes and devours. In both **Ezekiel 20:47-48** and **Jeremiah 17:27**, God's fiery wrath will not be quenched, meaning it will be unstoppable, unable to be extinguished. And because it will be unstoppable, it will "devour" trees and palaces; when describing fire, "devour" refers to completely burning up. And this idiom is used in the same way in the New Testament in **Matthew 3:12** and **Luke 3:17** in which John the Baptist says Jesus will burn the chaff with unquenchable fire. If the metaphor weren't clear enough, here "burn" translates a Greek word meaning to "burn up," "to consume completely."

The worm which will not die communicates the same point as the scavenging beasts and birds in **Jeremiah 7:33** and **Deuteronomy 28:26**, scavengers which cannot be frightened away from the corpses they feed upon, and so will therefore completely devour them.

I've saved for last the symbolism of the book of Revelation, which is frequently pointed to as support for the traditional view, when in fact it teaches something quite different. You need to keep in mind that as Richard Bauckham put it, Revelation is "a highly stylized form of literature, with its own conventions of symbolism and terminology…a literature of dreams and visions…never intended to depict the End in literal terms." (*New Bible Dictionary*, s.v. "apocalyptic.") Secondly, you need to keep in mind that, as G. K. Beale notes, "No other book of the NT is as permeated by the OT as is Revelation. Although its author seldom quotes the OT directly, allusions and echoes are found in almost every verse of the book." (D. A. Carson & G. K. Beale, *Commentary on the New Testament Use of the Old Testament* (Baker, 2007), Kindle edition, p. 1081.) Keep those two points in mind as we look at these passages.

Revelation 14:9-11 sounds like it teaches eternal life in hell; it speaks of smoke rising forever from the torment of restless beast-worshippers, but let's look at all the imagery and how it's used in the

Old Testament whence it comes: drinking God's wrath, fire and sulfur, and smoke rising forever.

Job 21:20-21 says, "Let their own eyes see their destruction, and let them drink of the wrath of the Almighty…their months is cut off." In the imagery of **Jeremiah 25:15-33**, where the nations are made to drink of the cup of the wine of God's wrath, God summons a sword against them, and their dead bodies won't be buried but will instead be dung on the surface of the ground. So drinking of God's wrath is associated with being slaughtered.

So, too, is the imagery of sulfur and fire, and rising smoke, imagery coming from **Genesis 19:24 and 28**, and **Isaiah 34:9-10**, in which fire and sulfur destroys cities and their inhabitants, and smoke rises forever from their remains. So this imagery, of smoke rising forever from torment, symbolizes death and destruction.

In **Revelation 20:10**, the devil, beast and false prophet are all tormented forever in a lake of fire and sulfur—there's that imagery symbolizing destruction again—and the unsaved are later thrown into it.

But this is the same lake of fire into which death and Hades are also thrown after being emptied of their dead (**Rev. 20:13-14**), and death and Hades can't be tormented at all. Death is the process of dying; Hades the grave or the underworld, the place of the dead. The imagery symbolizes an end to death and Hades—in fact, it symbolizes an end to, or the destruction of, everything thrown into it. This is why both John and God Himself interpret the lake of fire imagery as symbolism representing "the second death" of human beings thrown into it (**Rev. 20:14, 21:8**). "The second death" is not another metaphor; it's the straightforward, plain interpretation of the metaphors in the imagery. The unsaved will die a second time.

And so, when we look at "The Biblical Language of Destruction," we see that the Bible consistently, repeatedly, in no uncertain terms and in a variety of ways, says that as their punishment in hell, the unsaved will be destroyed, brought to a complete and irreversible end of life.

Conclusion

No doubt, many issues will be discussed in the course of tonight's debate, but I want to remind you now as I finish that the Bible is trustworthy, consistent and authoritative, and we must not read our presupposed view of hell into the text of Scripture. Rather, our understanding of any texts which touch on the doctrine of hell must be consistent: first with the answer to "The Biblical Question of Immortality," which is that immortality is only given to the saved; second, with "The Biblical Nature of the Atonement," which is that Jesus bore the punishment of death, and so the unsaved will bear that punishment themselves; and third, with "The Biblical Language of Destruction," which tells us that the lives of the unsaved will be brought to an end in their destruction.

A Defense of the Traditional View of Hell
Dr. Phil Fernandes

Introduction

It is an honor to be here tonight—defending the traditional view of hell as eternal conscious suffering. Though I wish harm on no man, I believe that the Word of God clearly teaches that Gehenna is a place where the unsaved will experience eternal conscious suffering.

My opponent and friend, Chris Date, is a brilliant and articulate evangelical who is attempting to convince the evangelical church to rethink hell and embrace doctrines more commonly associated with the Jehovah's Witnesses and the Seventh-Day Adventists. Chris believes that the Bible teaches conditional immortality—basically, annihilation of the unsaved. Rather than eternal conscious torment, Chris believes the unsaved will be raised on the last day and then cease to exist for all eternity.

It is my thesis that the evangelical church should not be quick to reject the traditional view of eternal conscious torment. I believe the majority of the church fathers were right to accept the doctrine of hell as eternal conscious suffering. I believe the Bible clearly teaches this. I also believe that if we evangelicals reject the traditional view, it will open the flood gates so that other traditional views will fall as well. I will show this tonight in the annihilationism of Chris Date, for he rejects other traditional doctrines as well. As a growing number of evangelicals reject the traditional view of hell, I strongly encourage believers to resist this trend.

Reasons for Accepting Eternal Conscious Suffering

1) The Church has taught for the past 2,000 years that hell is eternal conscious torment. A partial list of great Christian thinkers who have interpreted the Bible as teaching eternal conscious torment include the following: Justin Martyr, Irenaeus, Tertullian, Cyprian, Chrysostum, Ambrose, Augustine, Jerome, Athanasius, Anselm, Aquinas, Bonaventure, Martin Luther, John Calvin, Jonathan Edwards, John

Wesley, Charles Hodge, Charles Spurgeon, D. L. Moody, B. B. Warfield, Francis Pieper, Louis Berkhof, Lewis Sperry Chafer, Henry Thiessen, Walter Martin, and Francis Schaeffer. Contemporary evangelical theologians can be added to the list: Millard J. Erickson, Wayne Grudem, Charles Ryrie, J. I. Packer, R. C. Sproul, John MacArthur, and Norman Geisler. Virtually all segments of traditional and contemporary Christianity have embraced this doctrine: Roman Catholicism, Eastern Orthodoxy, Mainline Protestantism, and Evangelicalism. If we decide to reject this doctrine, we must have solid Scriptural evidence for annihilationism. Because the doctrine of hell as eternal conscious torment has been the teaching of the church for the past two-thousand years, the burden of proof lies clearly with the newer breed of evangelicals who desire us to embrace annihilationism and reject the traditional view.

2) The Bible teaches eternal conscious suffering. I believe the Bible unambiguously teaches the doctrine of eternal conscious torment. This can be seen in numerous passages. Although the Old Testament focuses primarily on temporal, earthly judgments, there are two Old

Testament passages that I believe deal with the issue of eternal conscious torment: Isaiah 66:22-24 and Daniel 12:1-2.

Isaiah 66:22-24—In this passage, Isaiah speaks of the final judgment. Using figurative language, Isaiah says of the unsaved—their worm does not die and their fire is not quenched. The rabbis of Jesus' day, as well as Jesus Himself, would later use these metaphors to describe the eternal conscious torment of the unsaved.

Daniel 12:1-2—Daniel, speaking about the end times, says that "many of those who sleep in the dust of the earth shall awake, some to everlasting life, some to shame and everlasting contempt." Clearly, Daniel believed that both the saved and the unsaved would be raised from the dead in the last days. He believed that the saved would be raised to an eternal existence characterized by "life." On the other hand, the lost would be raised to an eternal existence characterized by "shame and everlasting contempt."

In the New Testament, God's progressive revelation of the state of eternal judgment becomes even clearer. In **Matthew's Gospel**, Jesus speaks of hell numerous times. He calls hell "Gehenna," naming it after a garbage dump outside Jerusalem. He speaks of Gehenna as a place of "eternal fire" (**18:8; 25:41**). He says that hell is much worse than physical death by drowning (**18:6**). Jesus refers to hell as "a furnace of fire" and a place of "weeping and gnashing of teeth" (**13:42**). In Matthew **8:12, 22:13**, and **25:30**, Jesus says that evildoers will be cast outside, into the darkness, where there will be "weeping and gnashing of teeth." Hence, hell is a place of conscious suffering. At the sheep and goat judgment (**Matthew 25:31-46**), Jesus tells non-believers to depart from Him, and He calls them accursed ones. He sends them to "the eternal fire which has been prepared for the devil and his angels." Jesus makes it clear that the cursed ones will go into "eternal punishment," whereas His followers will go into "eternal life." Therefore, Jesus describes Gehenna as a place of eternal fire, eternal punishment, darkness, separation from God, and conscious suffering. Just as the life of the believer will last forever, the punishment and suffering of the unsaved will last forever as well.

In **Mark 9:42-48**, Jesus tells us to remove from our lives anything that causes us to stumble. For, it would be better to be without these stumbling blocks than to enter Gehenna, a place of unquenchable fire, a place where "their worm does not die and the fire is not quenched." Like many rabbis of Jesus' day (as attested to by the Talmud), Jesus quoted from Isaiah 66 to relate the concept of eternal conscious torment.

In **Luke 12:47-48**, Jesus states that, when He returns, some of the unsaved will be punished more severely than other non-believers. In **Matthew 11:21-24**, Jesus said that some cities would face greater judgment in the hereafter than other cities. Apparently, there are different degrees of punishment in hell. This is not consistent with the teaching that all the lost will cease to exist. For, if annihilationism is true, then all the lost will receive the same degree of punishment.

Paul states that, when Jesus returns, He will repay those who rejected Him with "eternal destruction away from the presence of the Lord" (**2 Thessalonians 1:8-9**). Hence, the lost will be separated from God for all eternity.

Jude speaks of false teachers and their final destinies by using these words: "for whom the black darkness has been reserved forever" (**Jude 13**). At Christ's return, the unsaved will hide themselves in caves and call upon the rocks to bury them due to their fear of God's wrath (**Revelation 6:12-17**). At that point in human history, lost mankind will know that God's coming judgment is far worse than non-existence.

John tells us that those who receive the mark of the beast will drink of the wrath of God in full strength. They will be tormented with fire and brimstone, the smoke of their torment rises forever and ever, and they have no rest day and night (**Revelation 14:9-11**). This contradicts the annihilationist view, for if annihilationism is true, then the lost will have rest forever—they will cease to exist. But, if the lost face eternal conscious torment, then there will be no rest for them throughout eternity.

Revelation 20:10-15 inform us that Satan, the antichrist, and the false prophet will be tormented day and night forever and ever in the lake of fire and brimstone. In fact, according to this passage, everyone who is not saved will be thrown into this same lake of fire. They will share the same fate and the same eternal residence as Satan and his demons (**Matthew 25:41**).

The Book of Revelation closes with the holy city, the New Jerusalem, coming out of heaven to earth. There, God's people will dwell with the Lord. However, outside the city, in the lake of fire and brimstone, reside the condemned. They remain outside the New Jerusalem and are not allowed to enter the holy city (**Revelation 21:8, 27; 22:15**).

Hence, the Bible teaches that the lost will be eternally separated from fellowship with God. They face a destiny of eternal flames. They will have no rest day and night. There will be weeping and gnashing of teeth in the eternal flames of hell. Hence, the Bible teaches that hell is a place of eternal conscious suffering—annihilation of the lost is not biblical. Annihilationism would never generate the scriptural metaphors used to describe hell.

3) Justice demands that we deserve the ultimate punishment. God is totally just, and justice demands that the punishment fit the crime. All sin is rebellion against the ultimately worthy Being (i.e.,

God). Hence, we deserve the ultimate in punishment. Eternal conscious torment is the ultimate punishment, not the cessation of existence. In fact, Jesus said of Judas, "it would have been good for that man if he had not been born" (**Matthew 26:24**). Clearly, hell is worse than eternal non-existence.

4) Eternal conscious torment is a great incentive to trust in Jesus for salvation. When I first trusted in Jesus for salvation it was because I believed that if I rejected Him I would face eternal conscious torment. If I thought annihilation was the fate of the unsaved, I probably would not have come to Christ. The real possibility of facing eternal conscious suffering is one of the greatest motivations for a person to come to Jesus for salvation.

5) Annihilationism is based on a faulty definition of the word "death." Traditionally, Christian theologians have defined "death" as separation or neutralization. Physical death is the separation of the body and the spirit (**James 2:26**); whereas, spiritual death is when our spirit is separated from fellowship with God. Annihilationists have incorrectly defined death as the cessation of existence. By doing this, whenever the

Bible speaks of hell as eternal death or destruction, they read into the text their faulty definition of death. Hence, they assume what they are supposed to prove.

Annihilationists also use a faulty definition of life. Eternal life does not merely mean eternal existence. "Eternal" describes the duration and "life" describes the quality of that existence. Hence, eternal death does not mean eternal non-existence. Instead, it means eternal existence that lacks the qualities of life and joy.

6) Many annihilationists have caved in to political correctness and the new tolerance. Chris has told me that he does not believe in annihilationism because he believes it makes God a kinder, gentler God. Chris has told me that he believes God would still be just if He chose to eternally torment the unsaved in hell. Still, in these post-modern times, there is an over-emphasis on tolerance. Numerous annihilationists have stated that they find the traditional view of hell unjust and abhorrent. We humans are experts when it comes to sin; we are not experts when it comes to justice. We should not allow our emotions or our faulty views of justice to determine our beliefs. Instead, we should accept what the Bible teaches about the hereafter.

7) Annihilationists have aligned themselves with suspect theological systems of thought: Jehovah's Witnesses, Seventh-Day Adventists, and Open Theists. Though this alone should not cause us to reject annihilationism, it should cause us to reflect more on the issue. Do we really believe that the Christian Church has been wrong on this issue for two-thousand years, while cultic and heretical groups were right all along? If the church has been wrong on this doctrine, what other doctrines will fall?

8) The rejection of eternal conscious torment logically leads, either directly or indirectly, to other aberrant doctrines (soul sleep, physicalism, and a denial of the traditional understanding of the Person of Christ). I believe my opponent, Chris Date, is a very logical thinker. I truly believe that his rejection of hell as eternal conscious torment has logically led him to reject any conscious existence in between death and the future resurrection (i.e., soul sleep). Chris' annihilationism has also led him to embrace physicalism (the denial of the existence of a non-material soul). And, I believe that Chris' view of death as cessation of existence will logically lead to heretical ideas about the Person and work of Christ.

Soul-sleep is the view that humans cease to exist after death and before the future resurrection. But, the Bible teaches that both the saved and the unsaved continue to have conscious existence after physical death and before the future resurrection (**2 Corinthians 5:8; Philippians 1:23; Matthew 22:23-33; Luke 16:19-31; 23:43; Hebrews 12:23; Revelation 6:9-11**).

Physicalism is the belief that man is only his body—there is no non-material spirit or soul. But this is not biblical. For, Scripture teaches that man is both body and soul or spirit (**James 2:26; 3 John 2; Matthew 10:28**).

What happened to Jesus between His death and resurrection? If Chris is right, then when Jesus died He ceased to exist. In fact, leading annihilationist Edward Fudge has admitted that he believes Jesus ceased to exist between His death and resurrection. However, traditional Christianity, based on solid biblical interpretation, teaches that Jesus is one Person with two distinct natures forever. He is fully God and fully man. This is called the Hypostatic Union. As God, Jesus is immortal—He cannot cease to exist (**1 Timothy 6:16**).

If Jesus really experienced death, and if death is annihilation, then Jesus ceased to exist between His death and resurrection. On this point, the annihilationist faces a dilemma. If only Jesus' human nature died, then God the Son did not die for us; only a human being died for us. This comes very close to the Nestorian heresy—dividing Jesus into two persons. However, if we do not divide the Person of Christ, and if the whole Person of Christ died, then God the Son ceased to exist between Christ's death and resurrection. God would not have been a Trinity for the time Christ's corpse lay in the tomb. Only two members of the Trinity would have existed during this time.

Either way, whether the annihilationist believes Jesus only died in His human nature (i.e., the Nestorian heresy), or if he believes the whole Person of Christ (both human and divine) died, if death means annihilation, then the traditional doctrine of Christ must be rejected. The doctrine of annihilation, in my opinion, logically leads to heretical teachings concerning the Person and work of Jesus. However, if one espouses the traditional view of hell and death, then no difficulty in the doctrine of Christ arises. For, the one Person of Christ, both human and divine, died for our sins. But, in the traditional view, death does not entail the cessation of existence.

Conclusion

In conclusion, I beseech the Evangelical Church to hold fast to the traditional view of hell as eternal conscious suffering. In my opinion, the church should reject annihilationism—it is not the view held by the church throughout the centuries, it is not biblical, and it leads to the rejection of other traditional Christian doctrines as well. Though biblical debate between Christians is always healthy, I encourage you to reject annihilationism for the reasons I have given above. As for me and my house, we will side with the traditional church and the way she has interpreted these Bible passages for two millennia. Therefore, I encourage you to accept the doctrine of hell as eternal conscious suffering and I beseech you to reject the doctrine of annihilationism.

Rebuttal to Dr. Phil Fernandes' Defense of the Traditional View of Hell
By Chris Date

Introduction

I want to start my first rebuttal by thanking my friend Dr. Fernandes for his kind comments about me in his opening presentation. I need to correct a mistake he made before responding to his arguments. He said my view and annihilationism mean the unsaved will be raised and then "cease to exist," but you may recall that I never made such a claim in my opening presentation. I said they would rise and then die, be killed, be executed—capital punishment. It is their *conscious* existence that will come to an end, because their souls will die with their bodies.

Dr. Fernandes wants to say that eternal life in hell is in some sense "death," but it's in bodies which were once dead and are raised back to life, and which will live forever. The difference between our views is not between existing forever and ceasing to exist; it's between living forever in hell, and being deprived of life forever.

So with that in mind, let's dig into the eight arguments Dr. Fernandes offered in support of eternal life in hell.

Church History

Dr. Fernandes argued first that "The Church has taught for the past 2,000 years that hell is eternal conscious torment," but this argument is simply mistaken. In the first century, "Some [Jews] believed that the wicked would be annihilated in hell…while others believed the wicked would be punished forever in an ongoing state of torment." (Francis Chan & Preston Sprinkle, *Erasing Hell: What God Said about Eternity, and the Things We've Made Up* (David C. Cook, 2011), Kindle edition, p. 54.) And as Douglas Jacoby notes, the early Church was diverse, too: "Even such a stalwart defender of infinite torment as John Walvoord admitted that there was diversity of opinion from the beginning of the Christian era." (Douglas Jacoby, *What's the Truth About Heaven and Hell?* (Harvest House, 2013), Kindle edition, locations 1716-1717.)

Dr. Fernandes included Irenaeus and Athanasius in his list of early Christians he thinks believed in eternal torment, but they did not. Irenaeus said God grants continuance and length of days forever and ever to the saved, but that the lost deprive themselves of continuance and length of days forever and ever. (*Against Heresies*, 2:34:3.) He was a conditionalist, and so, too, was Athanasius. He said that sin leads men back to the nothingness whence they came, and that Jesus died so that his people would not reap that consequence of sin. (*On the Incarnation of the Word*, chapters 6-8.)

Earlier in history was Ignatius of Antioch, who said that were God to reward us for our works, we would cease to be! (Mag. 10:1, in Philip Schaff, *The Apostolic Fathers with Justin Martyr and Irenaeus* (Wm. B. Eerdmans, reprint 2001), 63.) And of course there's Arnobius, who taught that the lost would be annihilated, too.

From the most recent several centuries, the list of conditionalists includes many names; I'm not going to take the time to list them here. You can find some of them in the EXPLORE section at www.rethinkinghell.com. Nevertheless, it is true that since the 3rd century or so, the traditional view of hell has been believed by the majority of Christians, but we don't determine truth by majority vote. There were conditionalists in the first centuries of the Church, and there have been conditionalists in recent centuries, including highly respected evangelicals like John Stott.

The Bible

Dr. Fernandes next argued that "The Bible teaches eternal conscious suffering," but this argument is still weaker than his first. Many of the texts he pointed to were texts which, as I demonstrated in my opening, are better support for my view. So I'll just address here the texts I didn't include in my opening.

In Daniel 12:1-2, the word translated "contempt" appears elsewhere only in Isaiah 66 where the corpses of the slain wicked are contemptible to the saved. Shame and contempt refer to how people are perceived. And note that Daniel is told that only the righteous will live forever, so the lost will rise to be judged and sentenced to death, forever remembered in shame and contempt.

Dr. Fernandes thinks annihilationism can't account for degrees of punishment, but that's mistaken. The final destruction of the lost may be by means that vary in type, intensity and duration of suffering, similar to the way in which death by the electric chair differs from lethal injection in how much suffering is inflicted.

In 2 Thessalonians 1:7-8, Paul speaks of "flaming fire" and "vengeance," language that comes from Isaiah 66:15, and in that chapter the lost are destroyed by being slain. "Eternal destruction" is an appropriate way to describe annihilation: the lost will be destroyed forever. Jude says "black darkness" has been reserved forever for the lost, but in Job 3, Job wished the day he was born had perished and become black darkness; it's an apt analogy for being deprived of life forever.

Justice

Dr. Fernandes argued thirdly that "Justice demands that we deserve the ultimate punishment." This argument isn't based on Scripture; it's purely philosophical speculation. But even if it's true, I believe annihilation is the ultimate punishment. I can think of no worse a punishment than missing out on eternal life with God. And it's interesting that our government and many others reserve capital punishment, not life in prison, as the penalty for the most heinous of crimes.

As for Jesus' statement in Matthew 26 that it would have been better had Judas not been born, of course it would have been! To have lived a life of sin, betrayed the Messiah into the hands of his murderers only to deeply regret and try to undo what he had done, to commit suicide, be raised from the dead, judged and suffer a violent execution, and be remembered forever in shame and contempt the way we remember Hitler, certainly is worse than to never have been born.

Evangelism

Dr. Fernandes argued next that "Eternal conscious torment is a great incentive to trust in Jesus for salvation." The reality, however, is that many people reject Christianity because of the traditional view of hell. Bertrand Russell and Charles Darwin rejected Christianity in part because they found the traditional view of hell to be repugnant. (Bertrand Russell, *Why I Am Not a Christian* (Simon and Schuster, 1957), 17. And, *The Autobiography of Charles Darwin 1809–1882*, ed. Nora Barlow (W. W. Norton & Company, 1993), 87.) Others reject Christ because eternal torment in hell sounds laughably absurd.

In his upcoming book on three views of hell, Steve Gregg talks about two people who were able to embrace Christ only once shown that the Bible doesn't teach eternal torment. (Steve Gregg, *All You Want to Know About Hell: Three Christian Views of God's Final Solution to the Problem of Sin* (Thomas Nelson, 2013, 63-65.)

Our understanding of hell must not be based on how we think it will be responded to. The Holy Spirit is the one who changes hearts and minds; our evangelism will have its greatest impact when the Spirit testifies to the truth of our message.

Faulty Definitions

Dr. Fernandes' fifth argument was that "Annihilationism is based on a faulty definition of the word 'death.'" This is simply false. We do not define "death" as "cessation of existence;" we define it as the Bible does, as cessation of life.

Dr. Fernandes cited James 2:26, in which James says "the body without the spirit is dead." When the body dies, we know what happens to it: it doesn't cease to exist, it ceases to live, ceases to be animated. The spirit, however, does *not* die, and instead lives on. But Jesus says in Matthew 10:28 that whereas men can kill only the body, God can destroy both body and soul in hell.

Political Correctness and Tolerance

Dr. Fernandes may be right when he says, as he argues next, "Many annihilationists have caved in to political correctness and the new tolerance." But as he notes, I did not. For now, I'll simply agree with him that we must accept what the Bible teaches about the hereafter, whether we like it or not.

JWs, SDAs, and Open Theists

Unfortunately, traditionalists too often employ the fallacy of guilt by association, as Dr. Fernandes does when he argues that "Annihilationists have aligned themselves with suspect theological systems of thought: Jehovah's Witnesses, Seventh-Day Adventists, and Open Theists." The reality is that more cultists and non-Christians believe in everlasting life in hell than embrace annihilationism.

Mormons, Muslims, Oneness Pentecostals, snake-handlers, the radical fringe of the Churches of Christ who believe in baptismal regeneration, the Westboro Baptist Church which despicably protests at soldiers' funerals saying God hates homosexuals; these and many others believe in eternal torment in hell—including many Open Theists! Of course, I wouldn't dare encourage you to reject the traditional view because cultists, Muslims and other non-Christians believe in it, and neither should you reject annihilationism because Jehovah's Witnesses believe in something like it. Jehovah's Witnesses also believe in monotheism and the inspiration of Scripture. Should we reject those doctrines? Of course not. As Dr. Fernandes said, we need to accept what the Bible teaches about the hereafter, regardless of who believes it.

Slippery Slope

Finally, Dr. Fernandes argued that "The rejection of eternal conscious torment logically leads, either directly or indirectly, to other aberrant doctrines (soul sleep, physicalism, and a denial of the traditional understanding of the Person of Christ)." But this, again, is mistaken. I began to lean toward physicalism or soul sleep before I ever began to question my belief in the traditional view of hell. Many conditionalists believe in the ongoing life of the immaterial soul after death. In fact, of the conditionalists we've interviewed on our podcast, more of them believe in the ongoing life of the soul after death than believe in soul sleep or physicalism.

But what of the atonement? Contrary to Dr. Fernandes' mischaracterization, my view is not that death is cessation of existence.

Jesus died—plain and simple. The hypostatic union was not broken; he continued to have two natures, and his human nature was dead. The doctrine known as the "communicatio idiomatum" explains that we can speak of the death of the one Godman, Jesus Christ, without requiring that his divine nature died in exactly the same way his human body died.

In reality, it is the traditional view of hell that comes dangerously close to heresy when it comes to the atonement. Traditionalists often say that the eternity of suffering which we would have faced was exhausted in the finite duration of suffering Jesus underwent on the cross. But if that's true, why did he go on to die? What penalty was left for him to pay with his death? The traditional view devalues the death of Christ, rendering it an afterthought, when it is the death of Christ which Scripture so emphasizes as the punishment he bore on our behalf! In conditionalism, on the other hand, he died so that at the judgment his people won't die. It's elegant, theologically consistent, and elevates the glory of the substitutionary, atoning death of Christ—as any understanding of hell ought to do.

Conclusion

So of the eight arguments my friend Dr. Fernandes offered, none of them holds up under scrutiny as being support for the traditional view of everlasting life in hell. The Bible teaches that immortality is given only to the saved, that because Jesus' substitutionary death is not accepted by the lost they will bear their own punishment of death, and that the lives of the lost will come to an end in their destruction.

Thank you.

Rebuttal to Chris Date's Defense of Conditional Immortality (Annihilationism)
By Phil Fernandes

Introduction

As you can see, Chris is a brilliant thinker who has done his homework. And he loves the Lord Jesus just as I do. Still, our differences of opinion concerning hell need to be addressed.

The Biblical Question of Immortality

In response to Chris' first argument—his argument from the biblical question of immortality, several things should be noted. First, I do not believe that the damned have immortality. I believe they will exist forever in conscious torment; but, this is not eternal life.

Second, eternal life is not immortality according to the Bible. Eternal life starts the moment a person first trusts in Jesus for salvation.

Immortality is when Jesus raises the bodies of believers—the perishable body puts on imperishability.

Third, I do not believe the unsaved will <u>live</u> forever. Chris is misrepresenting the traditional position on this point. I believe the unsaved will <u>exist</u> forever; but, that existence does not have the quality necessary for the Bible to refer to it as life. Believers receive eternal life; non-believers suffer eternal death. Eternal speaks of the duration—it will last forever. Life or death speak of the quality, or lack thereof, of this eternal existence. Hence, I would not say the damned "live forever."

The traditionalist believes that God only gives immortality to believers; the lost will be raised to suffer eternal conscious torment, but the Bible does not call this immortality—it calls it eternal contempt. The Bible teaches that the continuing existence of human souls is dependent on God; human souls are not eternal in their own power.

When speaking of humans, the Bible teaches that only believers' bodies will put on immortality at Jesus' return (1 Corinthians 15:50-57). Believers have eternal life from the moment they first believe (John 3:16; 6:47; 10:28; 11:25-26). But, biblically speaking, immortality only speaks of the believers' resurrected, glorified bodies. Non-believers will be raised, but not to life—their bodies will be prepared for God's eternal punishment.

The traditionalist believes God chose to create all humans with endless existence. But, God does not call the endless existence of the lost "life." He calls it eternal death, eternal contempt, and eternal punishment. God's Word speaks of hell as a place of weeping & gnashing of teeth, many lashes, eternal torment, no rest day and night, & eternal separation from God. Annihilationists confuse mere human conscious existence with life, but the two words, existence and life, are not synonymous. The church, for over a millennium, has never defined death as the cessation of conscious existence. The church has defined death as separation (i.e., the body from the soul and the soul from God), not annihilation.

The Biblical Nature of the Atonement

Chris' second argument deals with the nature of the atonement. Chris believes that, for Jesus to take our punishment for us, He had to die in such a way that He then had no conscious existence. But, this is not the case. The traditionalist defines death as separation, not annihilation or extinction. Hence, Jesus died for us in two ways. First, He died spiritually by being temporarily separated from the Father's fellowship—He was forsaken by the Father. Second, He died physically for us in that His soul/spirit departed from His physical body. The infinite, eternal Son was temporarily punished by the Father, in our place, so that we could be spared eternal punishment. Because of the worth of the Son, temporary suffering could atone for our deserved eternal suffering.

The Biblical Language of Destruction

In his third argument for annihilationism, Chris lists an impressive number of biblical passages which teach that the lost will be destroyed. But, he assumes that words like "perish," "death," and "destruction" must mean annihilation. However, this is not the case. Adam and Eve died the moment they sinned (spiritual death). Yet, they still existed. This is what the Bible calls spiritual death (Ephesians 2:1-5). Adam and

Eve immediately experienced shame, guilt, pain and suffering (Genesis 3). Being spiritually dead, they also would face future physical death (Genesis 5).

Jesus describes Gehenna as a place where there is weeping and gnashing of teeth, eternal punishment, and many lashes. John describes the Lake of Fire as a place of fire & brimstone, no rest day or night, and a place of torment day and night forever and ever. Paul describes hell as eternal separation from God

Hence, God's Word explains what eternal death, destruction, and perishing mean—eternal conscious suffering. Death means separation and neutralization (separation of body and soul; separation from God; thanatos—Vine—page 276). W. E. Vine says of the Greek word for destroy (apollumi), "the idea is not extinction but ruin, loss, not of being, but of well-being" (page 302). In fact, the Greek word for destroy (apollumi) is translated as "lost," referring to a lost sheep, a lost coin, and a lost son in Luke chapter 15. Destroy often does not mean annihilate. We must allow the Bible to tell us whether the flames of hell annihilate the unsaved or torment them. The Bible says the flames of hell torment the unsaved. Even though the biblical imagery of hell speaks of weeds being burned in fire, Jesus adds "in that place there shall be weeping and gnashing of teeth" (Matthew 13:40-42). Hence, being burned with fire points to conscious suffering, not annihilation.

Chris tries to lessen the impact of Revelation's passages concerning the Lake of Fire by pointing to the heavy symbolism of the Book of Revelation in an attempt to remove the sting of passages that teach the lost will have no rest day or night, and that they will be tormented (Revelation 14:9-11). He rejects the literal existence of the antichrist and false prophet when dealing with a passage that says that they, as well as Satan, will be tormented day and night forever and ever (Revelation 20:10). Though the Book of Revelation is filled with metaphorical language, I believe the unbiased reader will admit that it teaches that the Lake of Fire is a place of eternal conscious torment, not a place where the wicked are annihilated. In fact, in the last chapter of Revelation, after the new heaven and new earth have been established, the lost are still mentioned as existing outside the walls of the holy city (Revelation 22:15). Even G. K. Beale, who is quoted by Chris Date as an authority on interpreting Revelation, believes that Revelation teaches eternal conscious torment.

When Revelation says that "death and Hades" are thrown into the Lake of Fire, it merely means that the wicked are raised from their graves (i.e., death) and their souls are released from Hades, only to be condemned by Christ and thrown into the Lake of Fire. The fact that death and Hades are thrown into the Lake of Fire in no way means it cannot be a place of eternal torment. Chris' conclusion just does not follow.

My Response to Chris' Rebuttal

In regards to the history of the doctrine of eternal conscious torment, the great nineteenth-century scholar of ancient Judaism, Alfred Edersheim, made it clear that the two leading rabbinical schools (Hillel and Shammai) of Jesus' day both taught eternal conscious torment and a conscious intermediate state. It seems that Jesus had no dispute with these views when He spoke about hell and when He told the story of Lazarus the beggar and the rich man in Hades.

As far as the first few centuries of the church are concerned, I will concede the point that the early church was divided, or at least unclear, on the issue of hell. Though I disagree with Chris concerning the views of Irenaeus and Ignatius, I do agree that the issue of hell was not a completely settled issue until about the fourth century ad. Still, Christian scholar William Crockett believes that "during the time of the early Apostolic Fathers, Christians believed hell would be a place of eternal, conscious punishment" (*Four Views on Hell*, 65). Crockett also quotes from Ignatius and Irenaeus, arguing that they believed in eternal conscious torment.

I totally disagree with <u>Chris' claim that my biblical case for eternal conscious suffering is weak</u>. Most of the great thinkers throughout church history have agreed with my interpretation of these passages. I will let the passages speak for themselves. Each person in attendance tonight can decide for themselves whether the passages I have quoted teach eternal conscious torment or annihilation. As far as I am concerned, and most evangelical commentators agree with me, the passages I alluded to in my opening statement clearly teach eternal conscious torment.

The Bible's teaching that there will be different degrees of punishment in hell clearly favors the traditional position. For, if annihilationism is true, then Hitler and my nice unsaved neighbor will experience the same judgment—annihilation. But, if traditionalism is true, Hitler will be more severely punished than my neighbor.

As I said in my opening statement, the fact that Jehovah's Witnesses, Seventh-Day Adventists, and Open Theists espouse annihilationism should not be the sole reason why a Christian rejects annihilationism. But, I do think it should cause us to think twice about abandoning the traditional view of the church concerning hell. I agree with Chris that ultimately our understanding of God's Word should be the determining factor. Still, I find it rather odd that, if annihilationists are right, several cults got this doctrine right, whereas the church for the past 1,600 years got it wrong!

Though I am aware of many annihilationists who do not agree with Chris, I believe Chris' denial of the existence of a non-material soul and his denial that humans continue to have conscious existence between death and resurrection are the logical implications of annihilationism. I truly believe that if one denies eternal conscious torment and defines death as the cessation of conscious existence, then soul-sleep and physicalism logically follow.

Yet, the Bible clearly teaches that when a human dies, the soul departs and continues to have conscious existence. The soul of a believer goes immediately into God's presence:

--2 Corinthians 5:8 "prefer rather to be absent from the body & at home with the Lord").

--Philippians 1:23--Paul desires to depart (die) and be with Christ.

--2 Timothy 4:18—Paul knew that immediately after his death he would be in God's heavenly kingdom.

--Revelation 6:9-11—the martyrs in heaven have conscious existence (see also Revelation 15:2).

--Enoch & Elijah went to heaven without dying—they didn't cease to exist (see Genesis 5 and 2 Kings 2).

--Luke 23:43—Jesus told the thief on the cross "today you shall be with Me in paradise."

--Hebrews 12:23—"the spirits of righteous men made perfect" are in heaven right now.

--Matthew 22:23-33—Jesus said that Abraham, Isaac, and Jacob were still alive hundreds of years after their deaths and thousands of years before the yet to come resurrection.

The Bible also teaches that the soul of each non-believer enters conscious torment in Hades: the story of Lazarus the beggar & the rich man relates this truth (Luke 16:19-31). The *Liberty University New Testament Commentary* lists ten reasons why this is a true story and not a parable (i.e., personal names, etc.). But, even if it is a parable, Jesus still uses this parable to teach that both the lost and the saved will experience conscious existence between death and the future resurrection (NT scholar Craig Blomberg—*Interpreting Parables* & the ESV Study Bible notes).

Finally, since annihilationists believe that death is the cessation of conscious existence, then, for the God-man to have died, he would have had to cease to have conscious existence. But, if this is the case, then the

God-man would have ceased to consciously exist between His death and resurrection. I do not see how this does justice to the biblical doctrine of Christ as spelled out in the early church councils.

Conditionalism/Annihilationism
Supplemental Notes
By Chris Date

History of Annihilationism

Ancient Jews

Dr. Alfred Edersheim, based on what limited information he had available to him, may have thought the ancient Rabbis all believed in eternal conscious torment. But he died in 1889, over 50 years before the Dead Sea Scrolls were discovered. Today we know that Edersheim was wrong. "Some [Jews] believed that the wicked would be annihilated in hell…while others believed the wicked would be punished forever in an ongoing state of torment." (Francis Chan & Preston Sprinkle, *Erasing Hell* (David C. Cook, 2011), Kindle edition, p. 54.) The "Community Rule" found with the Dead Sea Scrolls says that those who walk in the way of the spirit of truth will receive everlasting life, but those who walk in the way of the spirit of deceit will face the "disgrace of annihilation...suffering and bitter misery in dark abysses until they have been destroyed." (Werner G. Werner, *The Manual of Discipline* (BRILL, 1957), 26.)

Early Church

Diversity existed among the early Church, too: "some believed in eternal torment, some in annihilation, and some in universal reconciliation." (Steve Gregg, *All You Want to Know About Hell* (Thomas Nelson, 2013), 108.) "Even such a stalwart defender of infinite torment as John Walvoord admitted that there was diversity of opinion from the beginning of the Christian era." (Douglas Jacoby, *What's the Truth About Heaven and Hell?* (Harvest House, 2013), Kindle edition, locations 1716-1717.)

Christians from the first and second centuries spoke mostly of the death that awaits the lost. Clement, in his first epistle to Corinth, says that the gifts of God to the saved include "life in immortality" (35:2) but that "vain toil…strife and…jealousy…leadeth unto death" (9:1). He tells us what he means by death, saying, "Enoch…was translated, and his death was not found" (9:3). The "death" to which sin leads, according to Clement, is plain in meaning. Ignatius of Antioch told the Trallians that Jesus "died for us, that believing on His death ye might escape death" (2:1). No code language here; the death Jesus died is the death from which believers escape, the death awaiting the unsaved. He wrote to the Magnesians that "were [God] to reward us according to our works, we should cease to be" (10:1). To the Ephesians he says the "one bread…is the medicine of immortality and the antidote that we should not die but live for ever in Jesus Christ" (20:2).

Early church fathers typically referred to final punishment using biblical terminology, without elaborating much in their own words. Sometimes, however, they used language of their own making. Irenaeus said, "It is the Father of all who imparts continuance for ever and ever on those who are saved … [they] shall receive also length of days for ever and ever. But he who shall reject it … deprives himself of [the privilege of] continuance for ever and ever … shall justly not receive from Him length of days for ever and ever." (*Against Heresies*, 2:34:3.) Athanasius said, "death having gained upon men, and corruption abiding upon them, the race of man was perishing; the rational man made in God's image was disappearing, and the handiwork of God was in process of dissolution." (*On the Incarnation of the Word*, 6:1.) He said that Jesus became a man and died in order that man would not "go to ruin, and turn again toward non-existence by the way of corruption." (Ibid., 6:4.)

Recent Centuries

There were conditionalists, then, in the early Church. So, too, have there been in recent centuries. Their names include (but are not limited to):

- **Isaac Barrow:** 17th century mathematician and theologian
- **Samuel Richardson:** 17th century pastor of the First Particular Baptist Church of London
- **Joseph Nichol Scot:** 18th century minister and author
- **Henry Constable:** 19th century Canon and Prebendary of Cork
- **Charles Ellicot:** 19th century Anglican Bishop
- **William Ewart Gladstone:** 19th century theologian and British Prime Minister
- **J. H. Pettingell:** 19th century Congregationalist author
- **Sir George Stokes:** 19th century president of the British and Foreign Bible Society
- **Richard Francis (R.F.) Weymouth:** 19th century Greek scholar and Bible translator

- **Basil Atkinson:** 20th century Greek scholar
- **E. Earle Ellis:** 20th century Professor at the Southwest Baptist Theological Seminary
- **R. T. France:** 20th century Anglican Greek scholar
- **Philip Edgecumbe Hughes:** 20th century Anglican clergyman and author
- **Dale Moody:** 20th century Professor at Southern Baptist Theological Seminary
- **Clark Pinnock:** 20th century theologian and lecturer at New Orleans Baptist Theological Seminary
- **John Stott:** 20th century renowned Evangelical leader
- **John Wenham:** 20th century Anglican biblical scholar
- **Richard Bauckham:** Professor at University of Cambridge
- **Jeff Cook:** Professor at University of Northern Colorado
- **Edward Fudge:** theologian, speaker and author of *The Fire That Consumes*
- **Michael Green:** Senior Research Fellow at Wycliffe Hall, Oxford
- **Gordon Isaac:** Professor at Gordon-Conwell Theological Seminary
- **Preston Sprinkle:** Associate Professor at Eternity Bible College
- **Douglas Jacoby:** Professor at Lincoln Christian University
- **Claude Mariottini:** Professor at Northern Baptist Theological Seminary
- **Christopher Marshall:** Professor at Victoria University of Wellington
- **I. Howard Marshall:** Professor Emeritus at the University of Aberdeen
- **Jim Spiegel:** Professor at Taylor University
- **John Stackhouse:** Professor at Regent College
- **Richard Swinburne:** Professor Emeritus at the University of Oxford
- **David Instone-Brewer:** Senior Research Fellow at Tyndale House

- **Greg Boyd:** co-founder and Senior Pastor of Woodland Hills Church

Death in Scripture

Physical Death the Consequence of the Fall

The warning in Genesis 2:17 that "in the day that you eat of it you shall surely die" may have meant that Adam and Eve died in a spiritual sense on the day they ate, but that's not all it meant. It further meant they had fallen under the sentence of physical death, and would inevitably physically die. Commenting on this verse, John Calvin said, "The miseries and evils both of soul and body, with which man is beset so long as he is on earth, are a kind of entrance into death, till death itself entirely absorbs him." Terry Mortenson at Answers in Genesis writes, "The Hebrew wording of Genesis 2:17 allows for a time lapse between the instantaneous spiritual death on that sad day of disobedience and the later physical death…As Scripture consistently teaches, both kinds of death (spiritual and physical) are the consequence of Adam's rebellion." (Terry Mortenson, "Genesis 2:17—'you shall surely die,'" *Answers in Genesis*, May 2, 2007.) And Mortenson notes that Paul, when appealing to the death that came as a result of sin in Romans 5:12, "is clearly speaking of physical death."

This is why God, following Adam's and Eve's sin, said, "By the sweat of your face you shall eat bread, till you return to the ground, for out of it you were taken; for you are dust, and to dust you shall return" (Gen. 3:19). He expressly revokes their access to the tree of life so that they would die: "'lest [man] reach out his hand and take also of the tree of life and eat, and live forever—'" therefore the Lord God sent him out from the garden of Eden" (Gen. 3:22-23). Physical death, included in the warning of Genesis 2:17, was a consequence of the fall, and Adam and Eve did eventually die.

Herman Bavinck said the curse in the first place brought about bodily death, suggesting that Genesis 2:17's "in the day" is used proleptically. Bavinck says this "places a close connection between man's death and his transgression of God's commandment...[and] is the fundamental thought of the whole of Scripture and forms an essential element in the revelations of salvation." (*International Standard Bible Encyclopedia*, s.v. "death.") He cites Romans 5:12 as one of several examples of Scripture identifying bodily death as the punishment for sin, and where Paul says in verses 13-14 that death reigned from Adam to Moses, Wayne Grudem correctly points out that "The fact that they died is very good proof that God counted people guilty on the basis of Adam's sin." (Wayne Grudem, *Systematic Theology* (Inter-Varsity Press; Zondervan Pub. House, 2004), 494.)

Spiritual Death

This "fundamental thought of the whole of Scripture" concerning the meaning of death serves as the basis for its metaphorical use, what is sometimes called "spiritual death." John Gill wrote that "the soul...is not capable of death, that is, in a natural and proper sense; it is capable of dying, in a figurative sense, a moral or spiritual death." (*A Body of Doctrinal Divinity*, book 7 chapter 2 (The Baptist Standard Bearer, 2001), 585.) Albert Barnes commented on Ephesians 2:1's "you were dead in your trespasses and sins," saying, "They were dead in relation to that to which they afterward became alive - i.e., to holiness...in relation to real spiritual life they were, in consequence of sin, like a dead man in regard to the objects which are around him." Herman Bavinck said, "The physical contrast between life and death gradually makes way for the moral and spiritual difference between a life spent in the fear of the Lord, and a life in the service of sin." (*International Standard Bible Encyclopedia*, s.v. "death.")

Cessation of Life, Not Existence

Biblically speaking, then, death is the loss or absence of physical life, and is sometimes used figuratively to refer to a life spent apart from God. Life is not mere existence, however, nor is death the cessation of existence. In Genesis 2:7, "the Lord God formed the man of dust from the ground and breathed into his nostrils the breath of life, and the man became a living creature." Evidently the man, Adam, existed when God created him, but he was lifeless. He began to live when God breathed life into him. When a person dies, "the life's breath returns to God who gave it" (Ecc. 12:7, NET), and he ceases to live. He is now a dead man.

Dualism and the Soul

What about the soul? Many conditionalists, including Seventh-Day Adventists, do not believe that human beings have non-physical souls or spirits that live on after the death of the body. However, many *other* conditionalists, such as Webb Mealy, David Reagan, and Robert Taylor, believe the souls of humans live on and remain conscious after the first death. But this does not change the meaning of death; death does not mean separation. Quite the contrary, it further establishes that death is the loss or absence of life, for James 2:26 says, "the body apart from the spirit is dead." When a person dies in this life, it is the body that dies, and the soul lives on. But in the second death, both die, for as Jesus said in Matthew 10:28, "do not fear those who kill the body but cannot kill the soul. Rather fear him who can destroy both soul and body in hell."

If the contrast between what men can't do and what God can weren't enough, the Greek word translated "destroy" (*apollymi*) consistently means "slay" or "kill" in the synoptic gospels in the grammatical form in which it's used in Matthew 10:28. As Glenn Peoples notes, "in *every single instance* of the word *apollumi* where these criteria are met – The example is in the Synoptic Gospels, the active voice is used and the word clearly refers to the actions of one person or agent against another, the term *apollumi* – setting aside Matthew 10:28 – always refers to the literal killing of a person, with not a single exception." (Glenn Peoples, "The meaning of 'apollumi' in the Synoptic Gospels," *Rethinking Hell* [blog], October 27, 2012. http://www.rethinkinghell.com/2012/10/the-meaning-of-apollumi-in-the-synoptic-gospels.) So in the first death, only the body is killed, and the soul lives on (assuming dualism); but in the second death, both body and soul will be killed.

Eternal Life in Hell

This is in stark contrast to the traditional view of hell in which, according to John Gill's comments on John 5:29, the lost "shall rise to life, to an immortal life, so as never to die more." The Belgic Confession says, "the evil ones … shall be made immortal." (Article 37.) John MacArthur says, "Every human being ever born lives forever;" ("The Answer to Life's Greatest Question, Part 1.") Greg Koukl and Christopher Morgan say that "everybody lives forever;" (Stand to Reason [radio], June 5, 2011.) Spurgeon said the lost will "live for ever in torment;" (http://www.spurgeon.org/sermons/0167.htm.) Gary Habermas and J.P. Moreland say that the unsaved "will continue living in a state with a low quality of life." (*Immortality: The Other Side of Death* (Thomas Nelson, 1992), 173.)

Dr. Fernandes claims his view is not one in which the risen lost are immortal and live forever in hell, but the words of traditionalists throughout Church history demonstrate otherwise. One can call eternal life in hell "death" if one wishes, but when a formerly dead body is raised alive from the grave and never dies again, eternal life is what it is.

The Book of Revelation

Although most traditionalists claim to agree that a sound principle of good hermeneutics is to interpret unclear passages in light of clear ones, they tend to interpret the vast wealth of biblical data concerning final punishment through the tiny, foggy lens that is the vision shown to John, recorded in the book of Revelation. Dr. Fernandes emphasizes this book as well, and for good reason: it's the only place which comes remotely close to promising eternal torment for human beings in hell. Although Revelation 14:9-11 says smoke rises forever, not that torment lasts forever, and although Revelation 20:10 says only the devil and two beasts will be tormented forever, nevertheless I agree that the imagery speaks of or depicts eternal torment. After all, the smoke rising forever must rise from something, and if the lake of fire is to be treated consistently, everything thrown into it should be eternally tormented along with the devil, beast and false prophet. But the question remains: What does this imagery mean?

Apocalyptic Imagery

There are those who seem to mistakenly think that John literally saw what was to take place in the future, as if it had been shown to him by the Ghost of Christmas Future. One author, for example, wonders "whether John saw some future technology to which he simply could not relate precisely and was only able to use the terms of his day to describe what he saw," explaining how modern helicopters may fit John's description of locusts with the tails of scorpions in Revelation 9:3-5. (Stephen Wood, *The Disciple's Guide to Revelation* (WestBow, 2012), 114-115.) But this simply is not how the vision of Revelation functions.

The book of Revelation falls within the genre of "apocalyptic" literature. Indeed, the genre owes its name to this very book. (*The HarperCollins Bible Dictionary (Revised and Updated)*, s.v. "apocalyptic literature.") Apocalyptic literature "comes through visions or dreams…that employ symbolic or figurative language used to describe a future divine intervention." (*Holman Illustrated Bible Dictionary*, s.v. "apocalyptic.") It is "a highly stylized form of literature, with its own conventions of symbolism and terminology…a literature of dreams and visions…never intended to depict the End in literal terms." (*New Bible Dictionary*, s.v. "apocalyptic.") To interpret the book of Revelation believing John literally saw the future, as if he watched a recording of it on a DVD sent back through time, is to completely miss its point and utterly fail to exercise the care necessary to properly interpret it.

A Rebirth of Images

The prominence that the OT is given in the book of Revelation is well known and acknowledged by scholars of all sorts. As traditionalists Don Carson and G. K. Beale put it, "No other book of the NT is as permeated by the OT as is Revelation. Although its author seldom quotes the OT directly, allusions and echoes are found in almost every verse of the book." (*Commentary on the New Testament Use of the Old Testament* (Baker, 2007), Kindle edition, p. 1081.) In the introduction to his parallel four views commentary on Revelation, Steve Gregg notes that the "symbols of the Book of Revelation are not generally novel or new, most of them having previously been introduced in other portions of Scripture. The book has been called 'a rebirth of images,' since it takes imagery familiar from hundreds of Old Testament passages and reworks them into new applications." (*Revelation: Four Views: A Parallel Commentary* (Thomas Nelson, 1997), 20.)

Because John's vision so heavily draws from the OT, one cannot hope to interpret the book of Revelation correctly without carefully considering what the language and symbols it records meant in the OT. John's epistle "cannot be understood without the Old Testament since it uses images from Exodus, Psalms, Isaiah, Jeremiah, Ezekiel, Daniel, and Zechariah" and "has parallels or allusions to most books of the Old Testament." (Kendell H. Easley, "Revelation," *Holman New Testament Commentary*, ed. Max Anders (Broadman & Holman, 1998), 12:2.) "This means that you can't take any of [John's] statements at 'face value,' because in general they will be composed so as to depend for their meaning on their relationship with a whole network of OT prophetic Scriptures. Try to read them without taking this background into account, and you can be guaranteed to misinterpret them." (J. Webb Mealy, *The End of the Unrepentant: A Study of the Biblical Themes of Fire and Being Consumed* (Wipf & Stock, 2013), 75.)

Interpretive Priority and Progressive Revelation

While the Holy Spirit has the freedom to use OT symbols differently in the NT, nevertheless he is "the same Spirit of prophecy that inspired the Old Testament penmen. And those Old Testament writings, more than any other literature of any description, are still our best guide to understanding the sometimes-bizarre characters and the often-puzzling events that this final book of Scripture lays before our blinking eyes." (Edward Fudge, *The Fire That Consumes*, 3rd ed. (Cascade, 2011), 236.) John did not merely exercise *carte blanche* creative license, repurposing OT language and imagery as he pleased in order to communicate whatever he wished. "This . . . fits poorly within the first-century Jewish milieu, where the integrity of a movement such as early Christianity would be judged by its coherence with the OT message." (Carson & Beale, p. 1088.) Yes, "'progressive revelation' is crucial in understanding the OT and John's book, as it is for all of the NT. On the other hand, of course, such 'progressive revelation' must not be separated from prior revelation, since it builds on and develops the earlier revelation with hermeneutical integrity." (Ibid.)

The Meaning of Revelation's Imagery

So what we have in the book of Revelation is symbolic imagery depicting or portraying eternal torment, but the meaning of that imagery, the reality which it symbolizes, must be carefully determined. As I explained in my opening presentation, Revelation 14:9-11 utilizes three images: drinking God's wrath, fire and sulfur, and smoke rising forever. And each of these three symbols feature in the OT as communicating death and destruction. Fire and sulfur is used again in Revelation 20:10, but that's not the only OT imagery which is reused here.

John's beast is the fourth beast from Daniel 7. Daniel's beast is preceded by beasts that look like a lion, a bear, and a leopard (7:4-6); John's beast has the appearance of a lion, a bear, and a leopard (13:2). Daniel's beast has ten horns (7:7); John's beast has ten horns (13:1). Daniel's beast is succeeded by the kingdom of the reigning saints (7:27); so, too, is John's beast (19:20; 20:4). But whereas Daniel's beast is slain and its body destroyed in a river of fire (7:11), John's beast is thrown alive into a lake of fire and eternally tormented (20:10). Taken literally, these two scenes are contradictory. However, the angel interprets the beast's fate in the fire for Daniel, saying it symbolizes the end to a kingdom's dominion (7:26). The NASB refers to its "annihilation." Likewise, the beast's fate in John's lake of fire represents the end to a kingdom's dominion.

Conditionalists can treat Revelation's lake of fire consistently as the end to, or the destruction of, the realities behind the symbols thrown into it. But this is very difficult for traditionalists. After all, death and Hades are thrown into the lake of fire, too, after being emptied of their dead (20:13-14). Death and Hades cannot be tormented in reality to begin with, though the fourth horseman of the apocalypse can (6:8), and its torment for eternity in the lake of fire symbolizes the end of death, the last enemy Paul says will be destroyed (1 Cor. 15:26). And John and God tell us that the torment of human beings in the lake of fire symbolizes their second death (20:14; 21:8).

Millennial Views

It's worth noting that, like traditionalists, conditionalists vary in their millennial views. Webb Mealy, David Reagan and Robert Taylor are all premillennialists. Edward Fudge and I, on the other hand, are amillennialists. Glenn Peoples is a postmillennialist. Focusing in this debate on differences concerning the millennium and Christ's reign will do nothing more than distract from the relevant and important issues.

The Person and Work of Christ

Based on his mischaracterization (surely an unintentional one) of my view as being that death means cessation of existence, Dr. Fernandes argues that if I'm consistent, I'm forced to say that Christ's humanity ceased to exist while he was dead. This, he says, either temporarily breaks the hypostatic union (if his divine nature lived on), or turns the Trinity into a Binity (if his divine nature ceased to exist with his human one). But as explained earlier, in my view death is the cessation or absence of life, not of existence.

Christ died, and was dead, during which time the hypostatic union remained intact. His divine nature remained united to his dead human nature. The doctrine known as the *communicatio idiomatum*, or "communication of properties," explains that something able to be experienced only by Jesus' human nature can be said to happen to the person of Christ, without effecting both natures identically. "Therefore," Wayne Grudem summarizes, "even though Jesus' divine nature did not actually die, Jesus went through the experience of death as a whole person, and both human and divine natures somehow shared in that experience. Beyond that, Scripture does not enable us to say more." (*Systematic Theology*, 560.)

So, contrary to Dr. Fernandes' claim, conditionalism does not lead to a denial of the orthodox understanding of the person and work of Christ. However, the traditional view comes dangerously close to heresy. When it is pointed out to traditionalists that Jesus did not suffer an eternity of torment in our place, they often say something like, "because of the infinite dignity of Christ's person, his sufferings, though finite in duration, were of infinite weight on the scales of divine justice." (Robert Peterson, *Two Views of Hell* (IVP Academic, 2000), 175.) According to many traditionalists, the finite duration of Jesus' suffering and anguish is the equivalent of the eternity of agony awaiting unbelievers on account of His divine nature.

But if this is true, why did Jesus go on to die? After he had fully exhausted the penalty of eternal torment owed to sinners in the finite duration of his suffering, what penalty was left to pay with his death? By equating Jesus' finite period of suffering with the eternity of torment they believe awaits the lost, at best traditionalists render his death a secondary afterthought, and at worst deny its atoning value altogether. Alternatively, a traditionalist might say Jesus' suffering and death together comprise the penalty he bore on our behalf, and that we shouldn't expect his experience to be identical to that of the lost in hell. But at best, this renders Jesus a quasi-substitute who bore a punishment that his people wouldn't have suffered in the first place.

In conditionalism, on the other hand, Jesus suffered and died so that his people would not suffer and die at the final judgment. He bore the death penalty so that they would not. Because his substitutionary, atoning death is not merited to the lost (either because, as Calvinists believe, he died only for the elect, or because, as Arminians believe, his free gift is rejected by the lost), they must bear that punishment themselves. Therefore, as he suffered and died, so, too, must the lost suffer and die at the final judgment. It's simple, elegant, and theologically consistent. It accounts for the biblical emphasis on his death as that which atoned for sin, and because Jesus actually bore the punishment his people deserved, he is their genuine substitute. Oh how the glory of the cross is lifted up in conditionalism!

Political Correctness and the New Tolerance

Dr. Fernandes believes that "Many annihilationists have caved in to political correctness and the new tolerance," but since he admits that I did not, I have not responded to this argument except to agree that we must believe what the Bible says, whether we like it or not. However, it is worth noting that although many conditionalists first began questioning the traditional view of hell because they found it morally repugnant or unjust (I did not), it is exegesis and their commitment to the authority of Scripture that convinces them of conditionalism. Consider the following words of John Stott:

"Emotionally, I find the concept [of eternal torment] intolerable and do not understand how people can live with it without either cauterizing their feelings or cracking under the strain. **But our emotions are a fluctuating, unreliable guide to truth and must not be exalted to the place of supreme authority in determining it. As a committed Evangelical, my question must be—and is—not what my heart tells me, but what does God's word say?"** (*Evangelical Essentials.* Emphasis mine.)

Recommended Reading

- Edward Fudge, *The Fire That Consumes*, 3rd edition
- Edward Fudge, *Hell: A Final Word*
- Steve Gregg, *All You Want to Know About Hell*
- Douglas Jacoby, *What's the Truth About Heaven and Hell*
- David Reagan, *Eternity: Heaven or Hell*
- Robert Taylor, *Rescue from Death: John 3:16 Salvation*
- Webb Mealy, *The End of the Unrepentant*

Hell Debate—Supplemental Notes
Phil Fernandes

1)Possible Rebuttal

A Response to Seven Common Arguments for Annihilation

1) eternal conscious torment makes God an immoral, unjust monster

  A) the late open theist Clark Pinnock used this argument

  B) it is based on a politically correct view of tolerance

  C) Chris Date does not use this argument—he acknowledges that God would still be just if He chose to eternally torment the unsaved (I respect Chris for his honesty on this point)

  D) I believe that sin against the ultimately worth Being (i.e., God) makes the sinner deserving of the ultimate punishment (eternal conscious suffering)

  E) all sin is rebellion against the infinite Being—it makes the sinner deserving of an infinite punishment

  F) praise God that the substitute sacrifice for our sins (i.e., Jesus) is ultimately worthy & the infinite God Himself

2) perish, death, & destruction must mean annihilation

  A) Adam & Eve died the moment they sinned (spiritual death)

  B) yet, they still existed (spiritual death—Ephesians 2:1-5)

  C) shame, guilt, pain & suffering, future physical death

  D) Jesus describes Gehenna as a place where there is weeping & gnashing of teeth, eternal punishment, & many lashes

  E) John describes the Lake of Fire as a place of fire & brimstone, no rest day or night, & a place of torment day & night forever & ever

F) Paul describes hell as eternal separation from God

G) hence, God's Word explains what eternal death, destruction, and perishing mean—eternal conscious suffering

H) death means separation & neutralization (separation of body & soul; separation from God; thanatos—Vine—page 276)

I) W. E. Vine—destroy (apollumi) "the idea is not extinction but ruin, loss, not of being, but of well-being." (page 302)

3) **fire does not torment; it consumes & annihilates**

A) according to Jesus, eternal fire causes weeping & gnashing of teeth, many lashes, eternal punishment

B) according to John, eternal fire produces no rest day and night, & eternal torment

C) the fire is not quenched & the worm does not die because the burning one continues to exist

D) we must allow the Bible to tell us whether the flames of hell annihilate or torment—the Bible says torment

4) **eternal torment is unfair; the punishment far outweighs temporal sins**

A) this was answered already

B) sin is rebellion against the infinite, ultimately worthy God

C) it makes the sinner deserving of infinite, ultimate punishment

5) **in the end, all evil will be annihilated** (1 Corinthians 15:24-28)

A) Paul says Jesus will turn the Kingdom over to the Father when He has defeated His enemies and conquered death

B) the result will be that God is all in all

C) whatever that means, it does not mean annihilation

D) Revelation 20, 21, & 22 speak about God's final victory over evil & the establishment of the New Heaven and New Earth

E) yet, these chapters make it clear that the lost will still exist in torment outside the holy city

F) Theologian Robert Peterson states that "God's being 'all in all' means that He reigns over the just and the unjust; it does not mean that only the former remain." (*Hell On Trial*, 176)

6) God only gives immortality to believers; the lost will cease to exist

A) actually, I agree that only believers will be given immortality

B) but, it is not immortality of the soul (Plato's doctrine)

1) Plato taught pre-existence of souls, no resurrection, souls are eternal in themselves

2) the Bible rejects the pre-existence of souls, future resurrection, & continuing existence of human souls is dependent on God

C) when speaking of humans, the Bible teaches that only believers' bodies will put on immortality at Jesus' return (1 Corinthians 15:50-57)

D) believers have eternal life from the moment they believe (John 3:16; 6:47; 10:28; 11:25-26)

E) but, immortality only speaks of the believers' resurrection, glorified bodies

F) non-believers will be raised, but not to life

G) their bodies will be prepared for God's eternal punishment

H) God chose to create all humans with endless existence

I) but, God does not call the endless existence of the lost "life"

J) He calls it eternal death, eternal contempt, eternal punishment

H) God's word speaks of hell as a place of weeping & gnashing of teeth, many lashes, eternal torment, no rest day and night, & eternal separation from God

I) annihilationists confuse mere existence with life, but the two words are not synonymous

7) <u>The Old Testament uses the same figurative language for temporary punishment—we should interpret the NT in light of the OT</u>

A) proper hermeneutics, due to God's progressive revelation, interprets the Old Testament by the New Testament, not the other way around.

B) who is the Messiah? The New Testament tells us.

C) who is the "serpent" of Genesis 3? Revelation 12:9 tells us.

D) what fate awaits the lost? Revelation 14:9-11 & 20:10 tell us.

E) Jesus tells us as well (weeping, gnashing of teeth, lashes)

F) a metaphor can change in meaning depending on the context

--serpent can mean Satan (Genesis 3; Revelation 12)

--serpent can be a symbol of Jesus on the cross (Numbers 21; John 3)

--serpent can be symbolic of wisdom (Matthew 10:16)

G) the metaphor "smoke rising forever and ever" could mean something different depending on the context

H) in the context of final judgment, it means eternal torment

2) <u>Church Fathers</u>

A) traditionalists and annihilationists tend to interpret the early church fathers differently

B) there may not have been a great unity of thought on hell

C) still, traditionalist scholars like Morey and Crockett believe the Apostolic Fathers believed and taught eternal torment

D) Morey (273-279) quotes Justin Martyr & Irenaeus as teaching eternal conscious torment & conscious existence between death & resurrection

E) Crockett (*Four Views on Hell*, 63-70, 172-173) states that

Ignatius and other Apostolic Fathers espoused eternal conscious torment

F) many believe that Arnobius (around 310 ad) was the first Christian annihilationist (Peterson & Morey)

3) <u>Edersheim on Hillel & Shammai</u>

--Dr. Alfred Edersheim was one of leading experts of the nineteenth-century on ancient Judaism

--his most famous work *The Life and Times of Jesus the Messiah*

--"On Eternal Punishment, According to the Rabbis and the New Testament" Edersheim argued that the two leading rabbinical schools (Hillel and Shammai) during the time of Christ believed in the eternal conscious torment of the lost

--Christ used metaphors that the rabbis of His day used to describe eternal suffering (unquenchable fire & undying worms)

--if Jesus did not teach eternal conscious torment, He would have used different metaphors than He did

--annihilationism would never have generated the scriptural metaphors used to describe hell

4) <u>Jewish Literature</u> (Morey, 119-128)

A) The Dead Sea Scrolls represent the library of the Qumran community; as such, it is a collection of Jewish literature

B) hence, numerous differing views of hell are discussed

C) still, the main pharisaical schools during Jesus' day believed in eternal conscious torment (Josephus; Edersheim)

D) both Josephus & Philo held to eternal conscious torment (Morey, 126)

E) the Babylonian Talmud calls Gehenna is a place of fire

(Ger 357), in which the wicked will be "punished for all generations"(RH 65). Gehenna "imprisons forever" (Ber 173).

F) *Judith 16:17*—"putting fire and worms in their flesh, and they shall feel them, and weep forever." (150-125 bc)

G) since many ancient Jewish writings (but not all) taught eternal conscious torment, if Jesus was an annihilationist, why did He use metaphors that were being used by Jews who believed in eternal conscious torment?

5) Reformers

A) though Martin Luther temporarily entertained annihilationism, he eventually returned to the traditional camp

B) virtually all the Reformers were traditionalists

6) Logic of Salvation

A) all sin is rebellion against the ultimately worthy Being (God)

B) all sin makes us worthy of the ultimate punishment (eternal conscious suffering)

C) God is totally just—He cannot forgive sin unless it has been paid for in full

D) if there is a substitute sacrifice, that sacrifice must be ultimately worthy (i.e., must be God)

E) the sacrifice must also have to represent man and must be able to die (must be a man)

F) hence, God the Son had to become a man to be our substitute Sacrifice

G) those who reject this sacrifice must still face the ultimate punishment—eternal conscious torment

7) <u>Death = Separation</u>

    A) in the Bible, death does not mean annihilationism or the cessation of conscious existence

    B) the Bible teaches those who physically die continue to have conscious existence (2 Corinthians 5:8; Philippians 1:23; Luke 16:19-31, etc.)

    C) in the Bible death (thanatos) means separation

    D) physical death = the soul is separated from the body

    E) spiritual death = the soul is separated from fellowship with God

    F) the second death = eternal separation from God

    G) Biblical Language scholars agree—Vine (276), Thayer, Lenski

8) <u>Destruction (Apollumi)</u>

    A) W. E. Vine—"the idea is not extinction but ruin, loss, not of being, but of well-being" (302)

    B) destroyed is translated "lost" in Luke 15 (a lost sheep, a lost coin, a lost son)

9) <u>Soul-Sleep</u>

--annihilationists who are consistent with their views (like Chris Date) also deny the existence of the human between death and the future resurrection (this is called <u>soul-sleep</u>)

--once again, they agree with the Jehovah's Witnesses and the Seventh-Day Adventists; they reject the traditional view of the church

--but, the Bible clearly teaches that when a human's body dies the soul departs and continues to have conscious existence

--the soul of a believer goes immediately into God's presence

--2 Corinthians 5:8 "prefer rather to be absent from the body & at home with the Lord"

--Philippians 1:23--Paul desires to depart (die) and be with Christ

--2 Timothy 4:18—Paul knew that immediately after his death he would be in God's heavenly kingdom

--Revelation 6:9-11—the martyrs in heaven have conscious existence (see also Revelation 15:2)

--Enoch & Elijah went to heaven without dying—they didn't cease to exist (see Genesis 5 and 2 Kings 2)

--Luke 23:43—Jesus told the thief on the cross "today you shall be with Me in paradise."

--Hebrews 12:23—"the spirits of righteous men made perfect" are in heaven right now

--Matthew 22:23-33—Jesus said that Abraham, Isaac, and Jacob were still alive hundreds of years after their deaths and thousands of years before the yet to come resurrection

--John 3:16; 6:47; 10:28—believers receive eternal life from the moment we first believe; though we will physically die, we will never spiritually perish

--the soul of the non-believers enters conscious torment in Hades

--Luke 16:19-31 (Lazarus the beggar & the rich man)

--Liberty University commentary list ten reasons why this is a true story and not a parable (personal names, etc.)

--even if it is a parable, Jesus still uses this parable to teach that both the lost and the saved will experience conscious existence between death and the future resurrection (NT scholar Craig Blomberg—*Interpreting Parables* & the ESV Study Bible notes).

10) Physicalism

--consistent annihilationists like Chris Date deny the existence of a non-material human soul; they believe man is his body & that when the body dies the man ceases to exist until the resurrection

--however, the Bible teaches differently

--3 John 2 and Matthew 10:28 teach a distinction between the body and the soul

--our spirits can exist separate from our bodies (Hebrews 12:23; Matthew 22:23-33; Philippians 1:23; 2 Corinthians 5:8; Luke 16:19-31; 23:43; Revelation 6:9-11)

--after God created Adam's body, he still had to make him spiritually alive (Genesis 2:7)

--physical death is when the spirit separates from the body (James 2:26; Luke 23:46; Acts 7:59)

--there is now scientific evidence against physicalism—Dr. Wilder Penfield's brain research—decisions are not made in the brain. Decisions are made in the non-material mind which then acts upon the brain (see Habermas and Moreland, *Immortality: the other Side of Death* and Robert A. Morey, *Death and the Afterlife*, 195-196).

11) Continuity of Personal Identity

--if humans cease to exist between death and resurrection, then there is no continuity of personal identity

--once a person ceases to exist, God would have to re-create him at the Resurrection—it would not be the same person

--the only way to retain personal identity would be if the soul of the person continues to exist between death and resurrection

12) <u>Eternal Torment/Conscious Suffering</u>

        --eternal contempt, eternal punishment

        --weeping and gnashing of teeth

        --worm does not die & fire is not quenched

        --many stripes, few stripes

        --no rest day and night

        --smoke of their torment rises forever and ever

        --tormented day and night forever and ever

13) <u>Person and Work of Christ</u>

--if Jesus really experienced human death, and death is annihilation, then Jesus' humanity ceased to exist between His death and resurrection

--but, if Jesus' divine nature did not cease to exist, if death is annihilation, then the divine Person did not really die for us—only His human nature died

--but, if that is the case, then God did not die for us (Nestorian heresy)

--on the other hand, if the whole Person of Christ (both human and divine) actually died (and if death is annihilation), then the second Person of the Trinity did not exist while Christ's body was in the tomb

--but, if God is immortal, then God the Son could not cease to exist

--the annihilation view leads to Christological & Theological heresies

--the traditional view generates no such problems—for God the Son to experience death for us, He had to become a man. Jesus physically died for our sins but in no way did He cease to exist.

--in one of Chris' debates on this subject he responded by saying that when Jesus died He continued to exist as a dead human.

--apparently, Chris Date wants to have it both ways. He wants to define "living" and "existing" as synonyms when referring to people. In this way, a person cannot suffer eternal death and still exist at the same time. But, everything changes when Chris speaks about Jesus. Chris says that after Jesus' death, when He ceased to live, he still existed as a dead human! All of a sudden, "living" and "existing" are no longer synonyms! This enables Chris to proclaim annihilationism while avoiding heresies about Jesus.

--Chris then says that Jesus ceased to have conscious existence

--so, I guess he means that Jesus continued to exist between His death and resurrection as nothing more than a human corpse

--most people would disagree

--we don't consider a corpse a dead existing human

--we consider a corpse the body of a dead human who is no longer there

--**for God to be able to die for us, death <u>cannot</u> mean annihilation!**

--for, God cannot cease to exist

--God could become a man & die for us

--but, death means separation, not annihilation

--Jesus, while on the cross, was separated (forsaken) from fellowship with the Father (spiritual death)

--His soul was separated from His body (physical death)

--but, He still continued to exist as the God-man

--it is only when we define death as annihilation that Christological problems arise

14) <u>Degrees of Punishment in Hell</u>

--the Bible says there will be different degrees of punishment in hell

--<u>Luke 12:47-48</u>

--however, if annihilationism is true then all the unsaved will receive the same punishment—the cessation of existence

--my kind next-door neighbor, if he doesn't trust in Jesus, will receive the identical punishment that Hitler and Stalin will receive

15) <u>Plato's Immortality of the Soul</u>

--if true, this would still be the genetic fallacy (claiming a view is false merely because it came from a bad source)

--traditionalists could accuse the annihilationists of getting their view from the Jehovah's Witnesses, the Seventh-Day Adventists, Open Theists, or from the postmodern overemphasis on tolerance

--however, there are many differences between Plato's view & the traditional view of immortality

--Plato believed souls exist in the eternal world of ideals

--Plato believed in the pre-existence of souls—they were never created

--he may have believed in reincarnation

--Plato believed that souls are immortal and indestructible by nature

--Plato also denied any future resurrection of bodies—the goal was for the soul to escape the prison of the body

--the traditional Christian believes the soul is eternal (not immortal since that only is used of the resurrection body of believers in <u>1 Corinthians 15</u>) because God chooses to sustain it in existence.

--the traditional Christian denies the pre-existence of souls & reincarnation—God created human souls

--Moses taught the continued existence of the human soul long before Plato taught the immortality of the soul (Genesis 5; Exodus 3; Matthew 22)

16) <u>Immortality of the Body vs. Eternal Life</u>

A) immortality of the body is given to believers when they are raised to immortality (1 Corinthians 50-57)

B) eternal life, on the other hand, begins the moment a believer first believes; it is eternal spiritual life (John 3:16; 6:47; 10:28)

C) Jesus said that those who receive eternal life never perish (John 3:16; 10:28); this only makes sense if He means they will never spiritually perish (since believers do physically perish)

D) but, Chris does not believe in the existence of the non-material soul or spirit

E) so if Chris is correct, Jesus is wrong—believers do completely perish in between physical death and the future bodily resurrection

17) Eternal Life vs. Eternal Death

A) eternal = the duration of that existence

B) life or death = the quality (or lack thereof) of that existence

C) it misrepresents the traditionalist to say that we believe the lost will live forever

D) we believe the lost will exist forever, but that is not the same as living forever

E) the lost experience eternal death, eternal torment, and eternal separation from God; these are not things the bible would refer to as life

18) Death Penalty

A) Chris says the death penalty is worse than life in prison; therefore, annihilation is worse than eternal conscious torment

B) but, I disagree with this for several reasons:
  1) we don't torture prisoners severely—if we did, the death penalty would seem merciful
  2) hence, eternal torment is worse than annihilation
  3) our prisoners live better than many people on earth
  4) their needs are taken care of
  5) many death penalty societies believe in life after death & future judgment (hence, what follows death is feared)
  6) death, in many of these societies, is not thought to be annihilation
  7) Chris assumes his definition of death when he uses this Argument
  8) if judgment is thought to follow the death of a criminal, then that helps make the death penalty more feared than life in prison
  9) but, if death is thought to be annihilation, and if we severely & continuously tortured prisoners, then the death penalty would not be considered worse than imprisonment—it would put an end to pain & suffering

19) <u>New Tolerance (Stott, Fudge, Pinnock)</u>
  --Clark Pinnock viewed eternal torment as unjust and sadistic
  --John Stott—"Emotionally, I find the concept intolerable." (*Evangelical Essentials*, 312-315)
  --we must be careful not to allow the postmodern emphasis on tolerance to influence our interpretation of Scripture
  --we are all influenced by our culture to one degree or another

20) <u>The Beast is not just an Empire, but also a Person</u>

--Chris does not believe the beast is a literal person in <u>Revelation 20:10</u>

--does he believe the false prophet is a person?

--he does believe that Satan is a literal person & the passage teaches that
      he will be tormented day and night forever and ever

--many Christian Bible scholars believe the beast of Revelation is a
      literal person, though the beast also symbolizes an empire

--the beast will be worshiped by the world & he blasphemes God

--the false prophet will build an image of the beast & place it in the
      Temple & command people to worship it

--concerning the number of the beast, it is stated that "the number is that
      of a man."

--the beast, the false prophet, and the dragon each have an unclean,
      demonic spirit (<u>Revelation 16:13-14</u>)

--the beast is called an eighth king (<u>Revelation 17:9-11</u>)

--Paul speaks of the antichrist as someone who performs demonic
      miracles, sits in the temple, claims to be God, & will be defeated
      by Jesus at His return (<u>2 Thessalonians 2:1-12</u>)

--therefore, there are excellent biblical reasons for believing the beast is
      a literal person, and that he, along with the false prophet and Satan,
      will be tormented day and night forever and ever in the lake of fire.

21) <u>Recommended Books</u>

--*Hell On Trial: The Case for Eternal Punishment*, Robert A. Peterson

--*Death and the Afterlife*, Robert A. Morey

--*Hell Under Fire*, edited by Christopher Morgan & Robert Peterson

--*Four Views on Hell*, edited by William Crockett

--*Two Views of Hell*, Edward Fudge & Robert Peterson

<u>Conditionalism/Annihilationism Passages</u>
by Chris Date

Unless otherwise indicated, all Scripture quotations are taken from The Holy Bible, English Standard Version. Copyright © 2000; 2001 by Crossway Bibles, a division of Good News Publishers. Used by permission. All rights reserved.

<u>The Biblical Question of Immortality</u>

Only God is by nature immortal. Human beings are mortal by nature, and by default will not live forever. Immortality is not universal. They can only receive immortality on the condition that God gives it to them as a gift through Jesus Christ (*conditional immortality*), and only then will they live forever. The unsaved, therefore, will not live forever.

Genesis 3:19

19 By the sweat of your face
   you shall eat bread,
till you return to the ground,
   for out of it you were taken;
for you are dust,
   and to dust you shall return.

Genesis 3:22-23

22 Then the Lord God said, "Behold, the man has become like one of us in knowing good and evil. Now, lest he reach out his hand and take also

of the tree of life and eat, and live forever—" 23 therefore the Lord God sent him out from the garden of Eden…

Proverbs 12:28

28 In the path of righteousness is life,
  and in its pathway there is no death.

Daniel 12:2

2 And many of those who sleep in the dust of the earth shall awake, some to everlasting life, and some to shame and everlasting contempt.

(The Hebrew word translated "contempt" appears elsewhere only in Isaiah 66:24, in which corpses are an "abhorrence" to those still living.)

John 3:16

16 For God so loved the world, that he gave his only Son, that whoever believes in him should not perish but have eternal life.

John 3:36

36 Whoever believes in the Son has eternal life; whoever does not obey the Son shall not see life, but the wrath of God remains on him.

John 10:28

28 I give them eternal life, and they will never perish…

Romans 2:7

7 to those who by patience in well-doing seek for glory and honor and immortality, [God] will give eternal life…

Romans 6:23

23 For the wages of sin is death, but the free gift of God is eternal life in Christ Jesus our Lord.

1 Corinthians 15:53-55

50 I tell you this, brothers: flesh and blood cannot inherit the kingdom of God, nor does the perishable inherit the imperishable. 51 Behold! I tell you a mystery. We shall not all sleep, but we shall all be changed, 52 in a moment, in the twinkling of an eye, at the last trumpet. For the trumpet will sound, and the dead will be raised imperishable, and we shall be changed. 53 For this perishable body must put on the imperishable, and this mortal body must put on immortality. 54 When the perishable puts on the imperishable, and the mortal puts on immortality, then shall come to pass the saying that is written:

"Death is swallowed up in victory."
55 "O death, where is your victory?
    O death, where is your sting?"

1 Timothy 6:15-16

15 ...the King of kings and Lord of lords, 16 who alone has immortality...

2 Timothy 1:10

10 ...our Savior Christ Jesus, who abolished death and brought life and immortality to light through the gospel...

Revelation 2:7

7 To the one who conquers I will grant to eat of the tree of life, which is in the paradise of God.

Revelation 22:1-2

1 Then the angel showed me the river of the water of life… 2 …on either side of the river, the tree of life…

The Biblical Nature of the Atonement

Jesus bore the punishment of hell in place of those who deserve it, as their substitute. The punishment Jesus bore was suffering and death. Therefore, those who must instead bear their own punishment will likewise be punished with suffering and death.

Isaiah 53:5-9

5 But he was pierced for our transgressions;
   he was crushed for our iniquities;
upon him was the chastisement that brought us peace,
   and with his wounds we are healed.
6 All we like sheep have gone astray;
   we have turned—every one—to his own way;
and the Lord has laid on him
   the iniquity of us all.
7 He was oppressed, and he was afflicted,
   yet he opened not his mouth;
like a lamb that is led to the slaughter,
   and like a sheep that before its shearers is silent,

so he opened not his mouth.

8 By oppression and judgment he was taken away;
    and as for his generation, who considered
that he was cut off out of the land of the living,
    stricken for the transgression of my people?

9 And they made his grave with the wicked
    and with a rich man in his death,
although he had done no violence,
    and there was no deceit in his mouth.

Romans 5:6-8

6 For while we were still weak, at the right time Christ died for the ungodly. 7 For one will scarcely die for a righteous person—though perhaps for a good person one would dare even to die— 8 but God shows his love for us in that while we were still sinners, Christ died for us.

1 Corinthians 15:1-4

1 Now I would remind you, brothers, of the gospel I preached to you, which you received, in which you stand, 2 and by which you are being saved, if you hold fast to the word I preached to you—unless you believed in vain.

3 For I delivered to you as of first importance what I also received: that Christ died for our sins in accordance with the Scriptures, 4 that he was buried, that he was raised on the third day in accordance with the Scriptures…

2 Corinthians 5:15

15 and he died for all, that those who live might no longer live for themselves but for him who for their sake died and was raised.

1 Peter 3:18

18 For Christ also suffered once for sins, the righteous for the unrighteous, that he might bring us to God, being put to death in the flesh…

The Biblical Language of Destruction

The Bible consistently, repeatedly, in no uncertain terms and in a variety of ways, says that the fate of the unsaved will be destruction, a complete and irreversible end of life.

Psalms

1:4 The wicked are not so,
   but are like chaff that the wind drives away.

1:6 for the Lord knows the way of the righteous,
   but the way of the wicked will perish.

2:9 You shall break them with a rod of iron
   and dash them in pieces like a potter's vessel.

37:2 For they will soon fade like the grass
   and wither like the green herb.

37:20 But the wicked will perish;
   the enemies of the Lord are like the glory of the pastures;
   they vanish—like smoke they vanish away.

37:38 But transgressors shall be altogether destroyed;
   the future of the wicked shall be cut off.

68:2 As smoke is driven away, so you shall drive them away;
as wax melts before fire,
so the wicked shall perish before God!

69:28 Let them be blotted out of the book of the living;
let them not be enrolled among the righteous.

Psalms (continued)

73:20 Like a dream when one awakes,
O Lord, when you rouse yourself, you despise them as phantoms.

104:35 Let sinners be consumed from the earth,
and let the wicked be no more!

139:19 Oh that you would slay the wicked, O God!
O men of blood, depart from me!

Isaiah 66:24, cf. Mark 9:48

24 And they shall go out and look on the dead bodies of the men who have rebelled against me. For their worm shall not die, their fire shall not be quenched, and they shall be an abhorrence to all flesh.

Unquenchable Fire: Jeremiah 17:27

27 But if you do not listen to me, to keep the Sabbath day holy, and not to bear a burden and enter by the gates of Jerusalem on the Sabbath day, then I will kindle a fire in its gates, and it shall devour the palaces of Jerusalem and (E)shall not be quenched.

Unquenchable Fire: Ezekiel 20:47-48

47 Say to the forest of the Negeb, Hear the word of the Lord: Thus says the Lord God, Behold, I will kindle a fire in you, and it shall devour every green tree in you and every dry tree. The blazing flame shall not be quenched, and all faces from south to north shall be scorched by it. 48 All flesh shall see that I the Lord have kindled it; it shall not be quenched.

Unstoppable Scavengers: Deuteronomy 28:26, cf. Jer. 7:33

26 And your dead body shall be food for all birds of the air and for the beasts of the earth, and there shall be no one to frighten them away.

Matthew 10:28

28 And do not fear those who kill the body but cannot kill the soul. Rather fear him who can destroy (*apollymi*) both soul and body in hell.

apollymi = kill: Matthew 2:13

13 …flee to Egypt, and remain there until I tell you, for Herod is about to search for the child, to destroy (*apollymi*) him.

apollymi = kill: Matthew 12:14, cf. Mark 3:6

14 But the Pharisees went out and conspired against him, how to destroy (*apollymi*) him.

apollymi = kill: Mark 9:22

22 And it has often cast him into fire and into water, to destroy (*apollymi*) him…

Matthew 13:40-42

40 Just as the weeds are gathered and burned with fire, so will it be at the end of the age. 41 The Son of Man will send his angels, and they will gather out of his kingdom all causes of sin and all law-breakers, 42 and throw them into the fiery furnace. In that place there will be weeping and gnashing of teeth.

Weeds Burned in an Oven: Malachi 4:1-3

"For behold, the day is coming, burning like an oven, when all the arrogant and all evildoers will be stubble. The day that is coming shall set them ablaze, says the Lord of hosts, so that it will leave them neither root nor branch. 2 But for you who fear my name, the sun of righteousness shall rise with healing in its wings. You shall go out leaping like calves from the stall. 3 And you shall tread down the wicked, for they will be ashes under the soles of your feet, on the day when I act, says the Lord of hosts.

Matthew 17:13-14

13 Enter by the narrow gate. For the gate is wide and the way is easy that leads to destruction, and those who enter by it are many. 14 For the gate is narrow and the way is hard that leads to life, and those who find it are few.

Philippians 3:19

19 Their end is destruction, their god is their belly, and they glory in their shame, with minds set on earthly things.

2 Thessalonians 1:8-9

8 …in flaming fire, inflicting vengeance on those who do not know God and on those who do not obey the gospel of our Lord Jesus. 9 They will suffer the punishment of eternal destruction, away from the presence of the Lord and from the glory of his might

Flames of Fire and Vengeance: Isaiah 66:15-16

15 For behold, the Lord will come in fire,
    and his chariots like the whirlwind,
to render his anger in fury,
    and his rebuke with flames of fire.
16 For by fire will the Lord enter into judgment,
    and by his sword, with all flesh;
    and those slain by the Lord shall be many.

2 Peter 2:6

6 by turning the cities of Sodom and Gomorrah to ashes he condemned them to extinction, making them an example of what is going to happen to the ungodly…

Sodom and Gomorrah: Jude 7, cf. Matthew 25:41-46

7 just as Sodom and Gomorrah…serve as an example by undergoing a punishment of eternal fire.

2 Peter 3:6-7

6 and that by means of these the world that then existed was deluged with water and perished. 7 But by the same word the heavens and earth that now exist are stored up for fire, being kept until the day of judgment and destruction of the ungodly.

Revelation 14:9-11

9 If anyone worships the beast and its image and receives a mark on his forehead or on his hand, 10 he also will drink the wine of God's wrath, poured full strength into the cup of his anger, and he will be tormented with fire and sulfur in the presence of the holy angels and in the presence of the Lamb. 11 And the smoke of their torment goes up forever and ever, and they have no rest, day or night, these worshipers of the beast and its image, and whoever receives the mark of its name.

Drinking God's Wrath: Job 21:20-21

20 Let their own eyes see their destruction,
    and let them drink of the wrath of the Almighty.
21 For what do they care for their houses after them,
    when the number of their months is cut off?

Drinking God's Wrath: Jeremiah 25:15, 33

15 …Take from my hand this cup of the wine of wrath, and make all the nations to whom I send you drink it.

33 And those pierced by the Lord on that day shall extend from one end of the earth to the other. They shall not be lamented, or gathered, or buried; they shall be dung on the surface of the ground.

Fire and Sulfur, Smoke Rising: Genesis 19:24, 27-28

24 Then the Lord rained on Sodom and Gomorrah sulfur and fire from the Lord out of heaven.

27 And Abraham went early in the morning to the place where he had stood before the Lord. 28 And he looked down toward Sodom and Gomorrah and toward all the land of the valley, and he looked and, behold, the smoke of the land went up like the smoke of a furnace.

Fire and Sulfur, Smoke Rising: Isaiah 34:9-10

9 And the streams of Edom shall be turned into pitch,
and her soil into sulfur;
her land shall become burning pitch.
10 Night and day it shall not be quenched;
its smoke shall go up forever.
From generation to generation it shall lie waste;
none shall pass through it forever and ever.

Revelation 20:10

10 and the devil who had deceived them was thrown into the lake of fire and sulfur where the beast and the false prophet were, and they will be tormented day and night forever and ever.

Interpretation of the Beast's Fate: Daniel 7:11, 23, 26

11 And as I looked, the beast was killed, and its body destroyed and given over to be burned with fire.

23 As for the fourth beast…
26 …his dominion shall be taken away,
    to be consumed and destroyed to the end…

An End to Death and Hades: Revelation 20:13-14

13 …Death and Hades gave up the dead who were in them… 14 Then Death and Hades were thrown into the lake of fire.

Interpreted as "the second death": Revelation 20:14

14 …This is the second death, the lake of fire.

Interpreted as "the second death": Revelation 21:8

8 …the lake that burns with fire and sulfur, which is the second death.

Eternal Conscious Torment Passages
By Phil Fernandes

Isaiah 66:22-24

New American Standard Bible (NASB)

[22] "For just as the new heavens and the new earth
Which I make will endure before Me," declares the LORD,
"So your offspring and your name will endure.
[23] "And it shall be from new moon to new moon
And from sabbath to sabbath,
All [a]mankind will come to bow down before Me," says the LORD.
[24] "Then they will go forth and look
On the corpses of the men
Who have transgressed against Me.
For their worm will not die
And their fire will not be quenched;
And they will be an abhorrence to all mankind."

Daniel 12:1-2

New American Standard Bible (NASB)

12 "Now at that time Michael, the great prince who stands *guard* over the sons of your people, will arise. And there will be a time of distress such as never occurred since there was a nation until that time; and at that time your people, everyone who is found written in the book, will be rescued. [2] Many of those who sleep in the dust of the ground will awake, these to everlasting life, but the others to disgrace *and* everlasting [a]contempt.

Matthew 18:6-8

New American Standard Bible (NASB)

6 but whoever causes one of these little ones who believe in Me to stumble, it [a]would be better for him to have a [b]heavy millstone hung around his neck, and to be drowned in the depth of the sea.

7 "Woe to the world because of *its* stumbling blocks! For it is inevitable that stumbling blocks come; but woe to that man through whom the stumbling block comes!

8 "If your hand or your foot causes you to stumble, cut it off and throw it from you; it is better for you to enter life crippled or lame, than [c]to have two hands or two feet and be cast into the eternal fire.

Matthew 13:42

New American Standard Bible (NASB)

42 and will throw them into the furnace of fire; in that place there will be weeping and gnashing of teeth.

Matthew 8:12

New American Standard Bible (NASB)

12 but the sons of the kingdom will be cast out into the outer darkness; in that place there will be weeping and gnashing of teeth."

Matthew 22:13

New American Standard Bible (NASB)

[13] Then the king said to the servants, 'Bind him hand and foot, and throw him into the outer darkness; in that place there will be weeping and gnashing of teeth.'

Matthew 25:30

New American Standard Bible (NASB)

[30] Throw out the worthless slave into the outer darkness; in that place there will be weeping and gnashing of teeth.

Mark 9:42-48

New American Standard Bible (NASB)

[42] "Whoever causes one of these [a]little ones who believe to stumble, it [b]would be better for him if, with a heavy millstone hung around his neck, he [c]had been cast into the sea. [43] If your hand causes you to stumble, cut it off; it is better for you to enter life crippled, than, having your two hands, to go into [d]hell, into the unquenchable fire, [44] [[e]where THEIR WORM DOES NOT DIE, AND THE FIRE IS NOT QUENCHED.] [45] If your foot causes you to stumble, cut it off; it is better for you to enter life lame, than, having your two feet, to be cast into [f]hell, [46] [[g]where THEIR WORM DOES NOT DIE, AND THE FIRE IS NOT QUENCHED.] [47] If your eye causes you to stumble, throw it out; it is better for you to enter the kingdom of God with one eye, than, having two eyes, to be cast into

[h]hell, 48 where THEIR WORM DOES NOT DIE, AND THE FIRE IS NOT QUENCHED.

Matthew 25:31-46

New American Standard Bible (NASB)

31 "But when the Son of Man comes in His glory, and all the angels with Him, then He will sit on His glorious throne. 32 All the nations will be gathered before Him; and He will separate them from one another, as the shepherd separates the sheep from the goats; 33 and He will put the sheep on His right, and the goats on the left.

34 "Then the King will say to those on His right, 'Come, you who are blessed of My Father, inherit the kingdom prepared for you from the foundation of the world. 35 For I was hungry, and you gave Me *something* to eat; I was thirsty, and you gave Me *something* to drink; I was a stranger, and you invited Me in; 36 naked, and you clothed Me; I was sick, and you visited Me; I was in prison, and you came to Me.' 37 Then the righteous will answer Him, 'Lord, when did we see You hungry, and feed You, or thirsty, and give You *something* to drink? 38 And when did we see You a stranger, and invite You in, or naked, and clothe You? 39 When did we see You sick, or in prison, and come to You?' 40 The King will answer and say to them, 'Truly I say to you, to the extent that you did it to one of these brothers of Mine, *even* the least *of them*, you did it to Me.'

41 "Then He will also say to those on His left, 'Depart from Me, accursed ones, into the eternal fire which has been prepared for the devil and his angels; 42 for I was hungry, and you gave Me *nothing* to eat; I was thirsty, and you gave Me nothing to drink; 43 I was a stranger, and you did not invite Me in; naked, and you did not clothe Me; sick, and in prison, and you did not visit Me.' 44 Then they themselves also will answer, 'Lord, when did we see You hungry, or thirsty, or a stranger, or naked, or sick, or in prison, and did not [a]take care of You?' 45 Then He will answer them, 'Truly I say to you, to the extent that you did not do it

to one of the least of these, you did not do it to Me.' [46] These will go away into eternal punishment, but the righteous into eternal life."

Luke 12:47-48

New American Standard Bible (NASB)

[47] And that slave who knew his master's will and did not get ready or act in accord with his will, will receive many lashes, [48] but the one who did not know *it*, and committed deeds worthy of [a]a flogging, will receive but few. From everyone who has been given much, much will be required; and to whom they entrusted much, of him they will ask all the more.

Matthew 11:21-24

New American Standard Bible (NASB)

[21] "Woe to you, Chorazin! Woe to you, Bethsaida! For if the [a]miracles had occurred in Tyre and Sidon which occurred in you, they would have repented long ago in [b]sackcloth and ashes. [22] Nevertheless I say to you, it will be more tolerable for Tyre and Sidon in *the* day of judgment than for you. [23] And you, Capernaum, will not be exalted to heaven, will you? You will descend to Hades; for if the [c]miracles had occurred in Sodom which occurred in you, it would have remained to this day.
[24] Nevertheless I say to you that it will be more tolerable for the land of Sodom in *the* day of judgment, than for you."

2 Thessalonians 1:8-9

New American Standard Bible (NASB)

[8] dealing out retribution to those who do not know God and to those who do not obey the gospel of our Lord Jesus. [9] These will pay the penalty of eternal destruction, away from the presence of the Lord and from the glory of His power,

Jude 1:13

New American Standard Bible (NASB)

[13] wild waves of the sea, casting up their own [a]shame like foam; wandering stars, for whom the [b]black darkness has been reserved forever.

Revelation 6:12-17

New American Standard Bible (NASB)

[12] I looked when He broke the sixth seal, and there was a great earthquake; and the sun became black as sackcloth *made* of hair, and the whole moon became like blood; [13] and the stars of the sky fell to the earth, as a fig tree casts its unripe figs when shaken by a great wind. [14] The sky was split apart like a scroll when it is rolled up, and every mountain and island were moved out of their places. [15] Then the kings of the earth and the great men and the [a]commanders and the rich and the strong and every slave and free man hid themselves in the caves and among the rocks of the mountains; [16] and they *said to the mountains and to the rocks, "Fall on us and hide us from the [b]presence of Him who sits on the throne, and from the wrath of the Lamb; [17] for the great day of their wrath has come, and who is able to stand?"

Revelation 14:9-11

New American Standard Bible (NASB)

[9] Then another angel, a third one, followed them, saying with a loud voice, "If anyone worships the beast and his image, and receives a mark on his forehead or on his hand, [10] he also will drink of the wine of the wrath of God, which is mixed [a]in full strength in the cup of His anger; and he will be tormented with fire and [b]brimstone in the presence of the holy angels and in the presence of the Lamb. [11] And the smoke of their torment goes up forever and ever; they have no rest day and night, those who worship the beast and his image, and [c]whoever receives the mark of his name."

Revelation 20:10-15

New American Standard Bible (NASB)

[10] And the devil who deceived them was thrown into the lake of fire and [a]brimstone, where the beast and the false prophet are also; and they will be tormented day and night forever and ever. [11] Then I saw a great white throne and Him who sat upon it, from whose [b]presence earth and heaven fled away, and no place was found for them. [12] And I saw the dead, the great and the small, standing before the throne, and [c]books were opened; and another [d]book was opened, which is *the book* of life; and the dead were judged from the things which were written in the [e]books, according to their deeds. [13] And the sea gave up the dead which were in it, and death and Hades gave up the dead which were in them; and they were judged, every one *of them* according to their deeds. [14] Then death and Hades were thrown into the lake of fire. This is the second death, the lake of fire. [15] And if [f]anyone's name was not found written in the book of life, he was thrown into the lake of fire.

Matthew 25:41

New American Standard Bible (NASB)

[41] "Then He will also say to those on His left, 'Depart from Me, accursed ones, into the eternal fire which has been prepared for the devil and his angels;

Revelation 21:8

New American Standard Bible (NASB)

[8] But for the cowardly and [a]unbelieving and abominable and murderers and immoral persons and sorcerers and idolaters and all liars, their part *will be* in the lake that burns with fire and [b]brimstone, which is the second death."

Revelation 21:27

New American Standard Bible (NASB)

[27] and nothing unclean, and no one who practices abomination and lying, shall ever come into it, but only those [a]whose names are written in the Lamb's book of life.

Revelation 22:15

New American Standard Bible (NASB)

[15] Outside are the dogs and the sorcerers and the immoral persons and the murderers and the idolaters, and everyone who loves and practices lying.

Passages that Refute Soul-Sleep & Physicalism

2 Corinthians 5:8

New American Standard Bible (NASB)

[8] we are of good courage, I say, and prefer rather to be absent from the body and to be at home with the Lord.

Philippians 1:23

New American Standard Bible (NASB)

[23] But I am hard-pressed from both *directions*, having the desire to depart and be with Christ, for *that* is very much better;

2 Timothy 4:18

New American Standard Bible (NASB)

[18] The Lord will rescue me from every evil deed, and will [a]bring me safely to His heavenly kingdom; to [b]Him *be* the glory forever and ever. Amen.

Revelation 6:9-11

New American Standard Bible (NASB)

[9] When the Lamb broke the fifth seal, I saw underneath the altar the souls of those who had been slain because of the word of God, and because of the testimony which they had maintained; [10] and they cried out with a loud voice, saying, "How long, O [a]Lord, holy and true, [b]will You refrain from judging and avenging our blood on those who dwell on the earth?" [11] And there was given to each of them a white robe; and they were told that they should rest for a little while longer, until *the number of* their fellow servants and their brethren who were to be killed even as they had been, would be completed also.

Enoch & Elijah went directly to heaven without dying—they didn't cease to exist (**Genesis 5; 2 Kings 2**)

Luke 23:43

New American Standard Bible (NASB)

[43] And He said to him, "Truly I say to you, today you shall be with Me in Paradise."

Hebrews 12:23

New American Standard Bible (NASB)

23 to the general assembly and church of the firstborn who are enrolled in heaven, and to God, the Judge of all, and to the spirits of *the* righteous made perfect,

Matthew 22:23-33

New American Standard Bible (NASB)

Jesus Answers the Sadducees

23 On that day *some* Sadducees (who say there is no resurrection) came to Jesus and questioned Him, 24 asking, "Teacher, Moses said, 'IF A MAN DIES HAVING NO CHILDREN, HIS BROTHER AS NEXT OF KIN SHALL MARRY HIS WIFE, AND RAISE UP CHILDREN FOR HIS BROTHER.' 25 Now there were seven brothers with us; and the first married and died, and having no children left his wife to his brother; 26 so also the second, and the third, down to the seventh. 27 Last of all, the woman died. 28 In the resurrection, therefore, whose wife of the seven will she be? For they all had *married* her."

29 But Jesus answered and said to them, "You are mistaken, not [a]understanding the Scriptures nor the power of God. 30 For in the resurrection they neither marry nor are given in marriage, but are like angels in heaven. 31 But regarding the resurrection of the dead, have you not read what was spoken to you by God: 32 'I AM THE GOD OF ABRAHAM, AND THE GOD OF ISAAC, AND THE GOD OF JACOB'? He is not the God of the dead but of the living." 33 When the crowds heard *this*, they were astonished at His teaching.

Luke 16:19-31

New American Standard Bible (NASB)

The Rich Man and Lazarus

[19] "Now there was a rich man, and he habitually dressed in purple and fine linen, joyously living in splendor every day. [20] And a poor man named Lazarus was laid at his gate, covered with sores, [21] and longing to be fed with the *crumbs* which were falling from the rich man's table; besides, even the dogs were coming and licking his sores. [22] Now the poor man died and was carried away by the angels to Abraham's bosom; and the rich man also died and was buried. [23] In Hades he lifted up his eyes, being in torment, and *saw Abraham far away and Lazarus in his bosom. [24] And he cried out and said, 'Father Abraham, have mercy on me, and send Lazarus so that he may dip the tip of his finger in water and cool off my tongue, for I am in agony in this flame.' [25] But Abraham said, 'Child, remember that during your life you received your good things, and likewise Lazarus bad things; but now he is being comforted here, and you are in agony. [26] And [a]besides all this, between us and you there is a great chasm fixed, so that those who wish to come over from here to you will not be able, and *that* none may cross over from there to us.' [27] And he said, 'Then I beg you, father, that you send him to my father's house— [28] for I have five brothers—in order that he may warn them, so that they will not also come to this place of torment.' [29] But Abraham *said, 'They have Moses and the Prophets; let them hear them.' [30] But he said, 'No, father Abraham, but if someone goes to them from the dead, they will repent!' [31] But he said to him, 'If they do not listen to Moses and the Prophets, they will not be persuaded even if someone rises from the dead.'"

About the Authors

Chris Date is the host of the *Theopologetics* podcast (theopologetics.com) and a contributor to the blog and podcast at *Rethinking Hell* (rethinkinghell.com). A software engineer by trade, he believes theology and apologetics are for every average Joe in the pews, and not just for pastors, philosophers, PhD's and the erudite in ivory towers. Formerly a traditionalist, he became convinced of conditional immortality over the course of a process which began when he interviewed Edward Fudge, and he has since defended the view in four moderated debates and on Justin Brierley's *Unbelievable?* radio program on Premier Christian Radio UK. Chris is married to his wife of over thirteen years, Starr, and has four boys ranging in age from twelve years to less than a month.

Phil Fernandes is the president of the *Institute of Biblical Defense*, the senior pastor of *Trinity Bible Fellowship*, and the Bible and apologetics teacher at *Crosspoint Academy*. His debates, lectures, and sermons can be downloaded from his websites instituteofbiblicaldefense.com and philfernandes.org.

Dr. Fernandes is married to his lovely wife Cathy. They have two grown daughters and three grandsons.